CAMBODIA

dos & don'ts

in Cambodia

By
Dr. David Hill

Illustrations by
Chan Vitharin and Chan Vanbora

ISBN 974-9823-10-9

Copyright © 2005 Book Promotion and Service Co., Ltd.

Published in Thailand by
Book Promotion and Service Co., Ltd.
2220/31 Ramkhamhaeng 36/1
Huamark, Bangkok 10240
Thailand
Tel: 66 2 7320243-5
Fax: 66 2 3752669
E-mail: publishing@book.co.th

Distributed by
Booknet Co., Ltd.
1173, 1175, 1177, 1179 Srinakharin Road
Suan Luang, Bangkok 10250
Thailand
Tel: 66 2 3223678
Fax: 66 2 7211639
E-mail: booknet@book.co.th

Printed and bound in Thailand by
Amarin Printing & Publishing Public Company Limited

Thank you for buying this book. We welcome your comments. Please send them to comments@book.co.th.

dos & don'ts in **CAMBODIA**

dos
&
don'ts

CONTENTS

INTRODUCTION

Cambodia

"Hey T.I.C. (This is Cambodia) Remember - what do you expect?" is a phrase you will hear often, and soon, after you arrive in Cambodia. It is also a phrase that you will probably find yourself saying as you soon take on the role of an experienced traveller giving advice to newer arrivals, in attempts to be philosophical and explain the inexplicable and unbelievable. Reports from Non Government Organisations (NGO's in their hundreds), the many UN offices, countless consultants as well as many travel books and learned treatises often contain the statement *"Cambodia is Different"*. "Well how so?" you ask. *"Well it's complicated"* you will be told, and read, and it is.

You will hear "hey T.I.C. trying to attract and rip off T.I.T. (Tourists in Thailand)", but this is too harsh, even if at least partly true, especially for those who come via road across the North Western border crossing from Aranyapathet to Sisophon in Bantey Meanchay Province. This is really the wild west of Cambodia with glitzy casinos providing much in demand gambling opportunities, with east European hostesses, for many thousands of Thais who cross the border daily. The wild west border areas are also notorious for smuggling and guns - hey you have been warned.

"There was a time not very long ago when Cambodia was referred to as the "Gentle Land of Smiling People" wrote Seanglim Bit, Ed.D. in the *"Warrior Heritage - A Psychological Perspective of Cambodian Trauma"*, which presents a psychological analysis of Cambodia written by a Cambodian scholar. Yet, as Dr. Bit notes, in the 1970's Cambodia exploded into world consciousness with the graphic horror of the most terrifying images produced anywhere in the second half of last century. How this slide into social disintegration happened, and how it can be reversed is the topic of countless discussions, studies, reports and also the focus of massive aid efforts which continue to gather momentum to this day.

Dr. Bit writes *"From an outsider's view, Cambodian culture and psyche seem to be riddled with shadows of contradictions and cross currents. At every step of discovery one is asked to reconcile what appears to be inconsistency between widely held fundamental social values and social behaviour. Outstanding personal attributes of loyalty, loving friendship, a joyful appreciation for life, etc., exist side by side with a darker, brooding intensity which can break out in callous indifference or intolerance of others."*

So we have contradictions and paradoxes.

In another odd consequence of the Khmer Rouge (KR) and war - the loss of cultural values amongst the Khmer allows them to be more open and approachable to foreigners. So whereas in Thailand

you may find that you are left alone and/or treated indifferently especially in rural areas, when you cross the border into Cambodia, people are friendly and welcoming and with a ready smile will say hello and ask where you're from.

This book is an attempt to present some simple advice for foreigners on **DOs** and **DON'Ts** when travelling in Cambodia. Some of the advice should be taken in a spirit of jest and with more than a grain of salt, but other advice is sincere and should be taken very seriously. There are more real dangers here than you are used to in your own lands, and to which you may not have the wherewithal to respond to in time. Foreigners have been killed because they didn't recognise some dangers and didn't respond quickly - whereas the locals that survived the KR and wars, know the dangers and have the reflexes to react quickly. An example of a life and death piece of advice relates to the presence of landmines especially along the Thai border in former combat zones. So off road adventurers take note - you **DON'T** want to lose a leg or a life.

This book is not a travel guide, a restaurant guide, a history book or a socio-anthropological text - there are ample of these - offering much worthwhile and worthless reading. This book is intended to give some advice on **DOs** and **DON'Ts** to help you have fun and leave in one piece with great memories and fond feelings for this "Different Country". Read on, take what advice you wish and enjoy. Remember *"IT'S UP TO YOU"* which may well be one of the first things you will hear from the Cambodian people when you arrive. How much for the taxi? - *"UP TO YOU"*.

So, **DO** expect to be surprised and amazed and **DON'T** lose your cool and sense of humour.

CAMBODIA
CURRENT CONTEXT

Cambodia

Cambodia is a Change Management Case Study par excellence and will remain so for the next few decades at least. The situation is very different to that in Thailand, and to Vietnam also for that matter. Whereas Thailand has never been colonised, has been experimenting with democracy for 60 years, has been at relative peace and has experienced sustained development for several decades, Cambodia has been governed by successive autocratic regimes since the early 1950's and been racked by savage wars for about 30 years. Cambodia today is seeing a great burst of reconstruction and the pace of change is fast.

Cambodia historically is a feudal society where an autocratic leader bestows benefits on his loyal subjects to ensure their support. Cambodia has had successive communist governments since the fall of South Vietnam in 1975 when the Khmer Rouge (KR) rose to power. After the defeat of the KR by Vietnamese led forces in 1979 Cambodia was a communist state under the control of Vietnam for 10 years. This was followed by a further 10 years of communist rule under the State of Cambodia. In 1993, after the UN sponsored elections, the country made a formal shift in policy to a "free market" based system but while this may be the official policy the apparatus of state is still locked in the old style of functioning.

On top of all this came and went the Asian economic crisis and the massive challenges of the internet age and modern communications. The traditional agrarian society based on the natural rich agricultural conditions in the country is changing as there is a great urbanisation and migration to the cities, especially Phnom Penh which is expected to double in population over the next 20 years or less. So today's Cambodia is very much in transition and does not have:

• A stable society with a unified sense of purpose and common national identity - some Khmer are great lovers of the King whereas others are not. Tragically Cambodia is a greatly fragmented society. Most Khmers have not travelled widely in their own country. One reason being that as recently as the early 1990's there was no freedom of travel - people had to get permission from the authorities to visit other provinces. So **DON'T** expect to find a strongly united people.

• Good security across the whole country, so do check out the advice of informed locals before jumping on a motorbike to explore the remote areas and **DO** take note of the dangerous mined areas along the Thai border.

• A national electricity grid, so **DO** expect power problems, especially out of the main cities (240v is the standard)

• A national banking system, so **DON'T** expect to be able to

use your credit cards and ATM cards as you can in Thailand.

• A good telephone system with national coverage and phone directories, so **DO** expect limited telephoning opportunities most

especially outside the big cities, although mobile phone coverage is increasing exponentially. Prior to 1992, Cambodia's international telephone system was routed via a Moscow operator.

• A good system of highways and national roads with reliable bus services, so **DO** expect transport challenges. Currently the Royal Cambodian Government is undertaking a major infra-structure rebuilding programme financed by the major donors.

• A reasonable health system providing access to quality health services, so **DO** take more care with your health and be more proactive and cautious than you would normally be.

• A good national education system. So **DON'T** assume that the Khmer people you meet with can read their own language - getting someone to write down instructions or your preferred destination in Khmer may not help if the driver of the taxi can't read.

Yet to some observers the more things change the more they stay the same. It is worthwhile keeping an open mind and keeping your eyes open. Cambodia is a fascinating place.

THE GREETING
or *"Sompiah"*

Cambodia

The polite form of greeting is the *"sompiah"*, similar to the Thai *"wai"*, hands held together as in prayer, head slightly bowed. The socially inferior, or younger person should be the first to move, but it is polite to

reply so fast that this is hardly noticeable. The higher the hands and the lower the bow, the greater the degree of respect. **DO** offer the sompiah to people of equal or higher social standing – not servants, waiters, taxi-drivers, etc. Monks should always be given a low *sompiah*, even if they are very young, since this respect is to Buddha. A monk will not return a *sompiah*.

Most educated Cambodians will follow western custom and shake hands with you. Yet it is still polite to *sompiah* first, before extending your hand. With women it is generally safer not to shake hands unless it is obvious that the woman knows western ways.

But all is not lost – luckily due to the French influence you will be able to greet some women (expatriate Khmer and the more westernised) with a kiss to both cheeks. So **DO** be French when it is appropriate.

When handing something over it is polite to use your right hand only. If the receiver is of higher social standing, you should support your right elbow with the fingers of the left hand.

KHMER SOCIETY

Cambodia

Only an arrogant or presumptuous person would attempt a summary of a culture in a paragraph or two. Yet many have tried especially driven by a desire to understand where Pol Pot and the KR came from. It is striking how many different views there are - it seems that foreign historians and experts are as divided as the Khmers themselves. Each writer has his/her own take. Therefore there are many fascinating books on Cambodia, its history, culture and people.

DO take the time to catch up on your history and knowledge of this ancient culture by reading a few of these books if history is your thing. Phnom Penh has several bookshops and supermarkets are also a good source of books. There are also many web sites with some focussing on sharing information and stories. The KR Documentation Centre has put all its information about the KR regime on the web.

Khmer society is complex and diverse and it does not seem adequate to sum it up in terms of two or more main pillars or characteristics, as has been done in neighbouring Thailand. The national motto is 'Nation Religion King' yet this is perhaps best understood as a goal or work in progress.

So how to sum up Khmer culture (in comparison with the cultures of Thailand and Vietnam) in a short, snappy sound bite? Here is one way. *"The Thais plant the rice, the Khmer watch it grow and sing love songs and the Vietnamese harvest it"*. Like all such simplicities there is more than a grain of truth to it. Yet this simple idea cannot explain the rise of the KR - where does the violence come from? Another metaphor is that the Khmers have a warrior heritage as descendents from the ancient days of Angkor with its kings and battles.

One way to get a picture is to see what well placed prominent Khmers and foreigners have to say. Recently, the then monarch, King Sihanouk was interviewed by Bernard Krisher, the publisher of the *Cambodia Daily* (the only daily Cambodian English language newspaper). The publisher was remembering his 40-year acquaintance with the former King. Krisher recalls that when he first met Sihanouk in the 1960s the King was presiding *"over a beguiling kingdom of glittering spires and French ballads, rice paddies and champagne parties. Cambodia really was a fairytale country in*

the 1960s. It had a King, it had a palace, it had beautiful streets. It had a nice, provincial, French atmosphere." He went on to say *"it had many people, educated in France, who provided art and culture and good food. I think people were very happy here".* While this may sound like an old colonialist hankering after the old days of the colonial masters, it is a sentiment shared by many Khmers who look back on this time with very happy memories and pride.

Krisher once asked the King how *"that sun-splashed Cambodia could collapse so quickly into the dark years of war. I said how could a person like Pol Pot emerge?"* Krisher says the King replied *"The Cambodians have a great sense of art and of taste, but there is also a great degree of cruelty in our culture. Cambodians can be extremely cruel. That facet was shown by Pol Pot."* Several of the top Khmer leaders were educated in France. Khieu Samphan at the Sorbonne. In the 60s Paris was a hotbed of Communist rhetoric. It's clear that the KR leaders learned much about the communist life from the French!

The British director Roland Joffe, who directed the famous film "The Killing Fields" offered another often stated perspective. In a recent interview in *The Cambodia Daily* he said *"But I look for a sense if there's a confidence. I think that's important. I think that the colonial experience in Cambodia was very destructive of the Khmer people's confidence in themselves. I think that's the worst price the entire colonial experience exacted. And that's one of the reasons that Thailand has had such a different experience as Cambodia."*

The rise of the KR has never been adequately explained and will not be explained simply in terms of US bombing, colonisation and divides between a poor peasant class and a corrupt urban elite. Why did the Khmers turn on themselves and kill their own kind so brutally? Some other frequently cited ideas are that there is a profound sense of fall from greatness amongst the Khmers who look back with pride and awe at the peak of Angkorian civilisation and wonder where it went. Some historians are damning in their critiques of the "God Kings" in the past and the perpetuation of a feudal society based on patronage and ever changing political alliances. Some argue that Cambodians are not ready for liberal democracy and that the "strong man" is the only style of leadership known. Others note that Cambodia lies on the religious fault line - "chasm or divide" between the Indianised Thai and Laos societies and the Chinese influenced Vietnamese.

There is a plentiful amount of material and an even more plentiful array of people with disparate views ready to argue their case. So if you are an armchair intellectual **DO** sit down in a café on the water with a coconut or beer as you please and discuss the state of things with your fellow travellers. **DO** be sensitive to your Khmer friends feelings if they are also in the conversation. **DON'T** be accusatorial or judgmental and make harsh criticisms.

Superstitions - ghosts, magic, talismans and charms

Cambodia is a land of magic - especially **BLACK** magic. **DO** beware of ghosts, the dark side and do keep talismans and charms to ward off the bad influences. **DON'T** forget to wear a lucky rabbits foot, sharks tooth or charm bracelet and keep a lucky card in your wallet. **DON'T** be surprised to see tattoos of astrological

symbols on some men, especially former soldiers - this saves them from bullets in battle. **DO** be sensitive to the feelings of your Khmer friends - they may be too scared to enter a building or go to some place because they fear the restless souls of the many who died there (especially in the KR period). **DO** know that the Khmer are highly superstitious so don't push your Khmer friends or mock their beliefs.

Ghosts, spirits, demons, bad dreams and omens bring much concern to many people. Many TV programmes feature ghosts and demons with lots of blood and horror. **DO** be sensitive to this and don't expect to be given explanations or to be able to understand. **DO** oblige if your Khmer friend wants to go to the pagoda to ask a monk for an explanation of a dream or to have a special ceremony performed to ward off some bad luck. There are special monks who have strong powers to overcome bad spirits.

DO expect the Khmer to be highly interested in your own ghost folklore, like haunted castles, Dracula and other ghouls and beasties. If you feel you would like an audience then do spin a yarn. There are many opportunities to have your fortune told by card readers and others. **DO** consult them if you are game.

As in other Buddhist countries people will wear Buddha pendants and these are afforded great respect - so do be sensitive to this.

Here is a list of some important **DOs** and **DON'Ts** about magic.

• Many ceremonies are held to ward off bad spirits and bring good luck. When people move to a new house or start a new business monks will be engaged to bless the premises or business. **DO** go along to your friend's house if invited to a ceremony of blessing.

• Every house will have a shrine called *"Neak Ta"* or "uncle Ta" and every time you go to the house do say a prayer. *"Oh please Neak Ta protect me and this house, and forgive me if I unknowingly do something wrong"*. If you don't do this you may be surprised to be punished for your sins. For example if you think the dark shady tree that the shrine is under is a convenient place for a discreet wee don't be surprised if you get an infection in the private parts. **DON'T** think you can fool uncle Ta. So do say your prayers and do be respectful of him.

• The famous "bodhi" tree that Lord Buddha gained enlightenment under is naturally associated with Lord Buddha and pagodas where they are mainly found. Yet the same tree is sometimes feared, as spirits will inhabit it. **DON'T** be surprised if people cut down or tear out young trees to prevent spirits getting a place to stay.

• Young women will often wear a white string around their waist with long cylindrical lead beads to protect their foetuses and prevent sickness. Monks put these on, or sometimes the girl's father, so **DO** respect them.

• Restaurants and shops also have shrines and Khmer and Chinese symbols above the door for good luck. **DON'T** make fun of these.

• The bloody streak down the mirror of the Chinese shrine in the restaurant above the menu board is indeed blood from some lucky persons tongue that was cut as part of Chinese New Year rituals. **DON'T** think about it - enjoy your food - just **DON'T** order tongue.

• **DON'T** be surprised if you see something that looks like a dead chicken or duck under a tree in your travels. It is in fact a dead duck and you are lucky. Dead black ducks are very good signs. Bad spirits will keep their distance. But keep your distance just in case it was unlucky enough to die from the bird flu.

• **DON'T** worry if you have a dream about a snake - it's a good omen. The woman or man you just met has feelings for you.

• **DO** be nice to three coloured male cats as they bring good luck.

• **DO** know that some animals have very special significance such as white crocodiles (their birth indicates major societal change), and white elephants (important symbols for the king).

• **DO** know that it is considered unlucky to close a business deal or buy a new house on Wednesdays.

• **DON'T** be surprised to see a dried cats placenta on the mantle in some houses. When a cat gives birth in a house and the placenta is not eaten it brings good luck. So people dry and keep them.

• If you want an adventurous, yet disturbing, shopping experience, **DO** take yourself off to a traditional medicine shop. Dried bats, dried testes and other animal parts as

well preserved medicinal plants, snakes, geckos and sundry animals clutter the shelves. **DO** your bit for animal preservation and speak out against the bits of endangered species you may find. On the positive side do shop for delicious herbs and spices. Cambodia is richly endowed with medicinal plants and herbs.

• **DO** be respectful of traditional medicine and traditional medical doctors - called *Kru* (derived from the Sanskrit word for teacher - "Guru") in Khmer. Many people consult them for mental and physical ailments. **DO** be open minded if you go along and don't be disturbed if the *Kru* spits on and rubs saliva over your face. Some western people report being helped in various ways.

• **DO** be careful accompanying macho men (like soldiers) to crocodile farms and the like, as they may want you to partake of cobra blood and whisky as an aphrodisiac. Bats blood in wine is also considered a great tonic. Eating dog also improves circulation and sex drive. But the best may be the $5 viagra at the local pharmacy - at least you won't have a queasy tummy.

SOCIAL CUSTOMS

Cambodia

Most Buddhist customs appropriate in other parts of the world and in neighbouring Thailand apply in Cambodia. However in every day life, Cambodia is less formal than Thailand especially in Phnom Penh and larger provincial towns. **DO** treat older people with more respect.

Modesty

Cambodians are modest in many ways and there are appropriate ways in which men and women should relate to each other. Signs of public affection between the sexes are inappropriate, but it is common to see men holding

hands with men and women with women. You may even see soldiers with AK47 strapped across their chests walking hand in hand while on a security mission for a high Government official. Men should not touch women in affection in public and obviously should not touch nuns – duh!! So a western couple should not have a passionate kiss on the main boulevard. It will draw disapproving glances (while inside the onlookers secretly enjoy the spectacle) and confirm that all western women are 'easy'.

Ladies **DON'T** wear sexy short shorts in public such as when you go jogging. If you understand Khmer you will hear people say – "wow look at her bum!" Clothing should also be modest and not revealing, especially in temples or *wats*. While travelling around Cambodia you will notice that women do not wear revealing clothing. The traditional Khmer attire includes a scarf or *krama* woven from cotton that is wrapped around the head and neck. This is extremely practical and worth copying as travelling in Cambodia often means sitting in overcrowded taxis or motorbike trailers with the wind and dust (or rain in the wet season) in your hair and eyes and the fierce heat of the sun beating down. So **DO**, as the locals do – wear a *krama*. *Krama* are often one of the first purchases of tourists in Cambodia - they are cheap, colourful and very useful.

Men: **DON'T** touch any part of a woman's body and **DON'T** stand too close to her or look straight into her face. Any of these will make the woman feel very uncomfortable.

Here are some other tips for romantic moments. Fellas, **DON'T** walk holding hands with your Khmer girlfriend. She is likely to feel very uncomfortable and will be subjected to jibes and

comments from passers by. Khmers will turn a blind eye to hanky panky behind draped curtains at the many popular picnic places at lakes and parks at which you rent a little bamboo shelter on the waters edge to eat out with friends. So **DO** keep the curtain drawn – and **DON'T** be surprised by a swarm of giggling curious children.

The smile and body language

Khmers have wonderfully radiant smiles that make their faces glow. Their deep brown skin colour can really accentuate their toothy smiles which make you feel good and at ease. Khmers also respond cheerfully to a smile. In fact, the smiles of the Khmers are one of the most frequently mentioned experiences noted by foreigners.

But note that the Khmers have two types of smile. One indicates pleasure, while the other shows embarrassment, and sometimes, guilt. This is why a Khmer will often smile broadly when imparting some bad news, something which foreigners may find absolutely maddening. So **DON'T** be shocked if a colleague when narrating the results of a tragic traffic accident, smiles broadly as she describes how someone is lying and dying in the road - it happens.

Here is a true story.

My office assistant borrowed a motorbike for a weekend to visit his family in a northern province. He didn't ask. When he returned there was no motorbike. I was angry because he had taken the motorbike without permission. I confronted him and he smiled broadly as he told me he had taken it. The smile infuriated me. His smile grew in size as he went on to say that he was even more sorry as the bike had been stolen from his cousins' house. I lost it and got very angry - should I make him pay it back or not? - more smiles.

Don't point directly at someone

As in other Buddhist countries it is regarded as extremely impolite to point your finger directly at a person. It is also rude to touch somebody on the head or hair.

Beckoning

To attract attention **DON'T** beckon in the western style, but hold your hand palm downwards with the fingers pointing towards the ground and waggle them loosely. When driving motorbikes **DO** indicate your intention to turn by putting out your arm in the direction of turning with palm down – if your are really serious and want to indicate strongly, straighten your arm and hand and waggle with gusto!

Body language - feet

DON'T point the soles of your feet at anybody as it is rude. When at a pagoda or dining at

your friends house **DON'T** sit cross legged but sit with your feet tucked back behind. It *is* uncomfortable so you can change your position as numbness sets in. At your friends home if it is too uncomfortable, smile and ask if you can sit cross legged and they will usually say OK. Or say you have bad knees and they will bring you a chair and a small table for your plate. At the *wat* though you will have to endure the pain and keep those soles pointed away from the monks.

Cleanliness and smartness

The Khmer love to dress formally and to look their very best, especially when they go out to dinner at a restaurant or visit friends or promenade along the river or in a park. In particular, the Khmer love to dress up their children with very pretty party dresses and suits. This is opposite to the western preference of dressing down into smart casuals to go out with friends. **DO** dress up if you want to mix with your friends and have a happy time. You are a rich foreigner - dress like one.

Yet the Khmer also have a very practical and clear sense of changing clothes into work attire for work in the field, and also when relaxing after meals. Thus men will often take off their shirts after meals at home or at picnic places and sometimes even their trousers and wrap a larger *krama* around their waist to sleep. Women unfortunately are not given the same freedom but can certainly loosen their shirt/blouse and other clothing to get cool when they want to rest.

The western short shorts are completely inappropriate for some obvious and practical reasons as they offend local sensibilities, offer insufficient protection from the trials of travel and most importantly leave your thighs, calves and lower legs highly vulnerable to very painful and severe burns from hot motorbike exhaust pipes – ladies be especially aware. **DO** watch out for the exhaust pipe – spend some time looking at the burns on Khmer girls lower legs.

Nature calls

Nature calls are no problem when travelling or when you are out in the countryside or rural areas, as the Khmer will simply avert their gaze and look away. Men are able to urinate publicly against trees, walls of building, power poles, etc. In fact it is quite a feature of travel to see people taking bathroom breaks *en route*. Prolific, ubiquitous public urination by men and public toilets (or lack of them) became an election issue in the 1998 election. Women are advised to carry a sarong (or you can use a towel) and wrap it around you and squat in a nearby discreet place - don't worry if it is not possible to find a completely quiet place as people will look away and the Khmer women are sympathetic. The

Khmer don't use toilet paper and will wash themselves in a river or stream or use a water pot if one is provided. So do carry some toilet paper with you tucked in your bra. Toilet paper is readily available at restaurants where it is used in place of serviettes.

Displays of anger

DON'T DO IT - NEVER DO IT - A MAJOR MISTAKE

It is regarded as impolite to speak loudly or to show anger or any form of violent behaviour. Try and smile before you speak. Whatever the situation, the foreigner is advised to keep smiling at all times!! So **DON'T** ever shout and scream. **DON'T** swear and abuse people, especially those friendly corrupt policemen at traffic corners. As in any other Buddhist country displays of anger are a sign of lack of control. But **DO** expect to have your self control challenged at times and **DO** remember your breathing - slow deep breaths in and out.

Another tip: **DON'T** write in red ink - are you angry with me?

DON'T ever strike a child on the head

NEVER, NEVER, NEVER, strike a child on the head - possibly the worst social offence you can ever commit.

True story:

I was at a popular picnic site with my Cambodian wife and our children as well as assorted family members, most notably some naughty young nephews. The boys started throwing stones at a cow that was grazing nearby and I asked them repeatedly to stop as the stones got bigger and were thrown harder. They didn't listen and kept throwing stones. So I walked over and tried to hit them in a not too hard manner with the palm of my hand. Just as my hand connected one boy ducked and the result was a hard slap to his head. The child cried and my wife (who never shouts even when we are in private) started screaming furiously at me. Everyone was looking - she screamed and screamed at me shouting that in Cambodia people don't care about animals and that I should never hit a child on the head. I was in the doghouse for months and only recovered my social acceptance after repeated apologies and gestures of friendship. Take note.

However, there are many games, especially Khmer New Year games (*see page 117*) when you can throw pillows and the like with great force and try to wallop someone. In a traditional Khmer game played with the seeds of the sugar palm fruit, smiling girls beat the crap out of boys and men's knees. So when playing boisterous traditional Khmer New Year games **DO** join in and wallop the girls with the pillow.

Silence means "No"

Cambodians do not like to say "no" and will really avoid saying it. This means there is a "yes", which is the affirmative and a "yes" which is a polite way of saying "no". A hesitant "yes" could mean "no". Silence means a definite no and that the person dissociates him/herself from the issue completely. If it is something important, try and find out the real "yes" but **DON'T** push the issue so the person becomes embarrassed or loses face. Sometimes people will say "yes" to please you or to make you happy but really it should be understood as "no". Remember **DO** keep smiling - and **DON'T** forget your breathing.

SACRED WATERS

Cambodia

Water is sacred and at the heart of Cambodia. Water is intimately imbibed in everything about Cambodia - seasonal routines and daily life, love, birth, food, religion. Plentiful water is the source of the rich agricultural foundation of the country and is part of the Khmer spirit and daily life. Water, in excess or lack of, affects and controls perhaps most, if not all aspects of life. The ancient city of Angkor was essentially an hydrological metropolis. Water was its base and its survival. Declining water was part of its downfall.

DO make an effort to appreciate the sacred waters of Cambodia - look at the classic image of the "Churning of the Ocean of Life" on the bas relief of Angkor Wat. This is the eternal tug of war between the Gods and Demons with the maintainer of the universe - Vishnu - in the middle. At the bottom there is water filled with crocodiles and in the sky are the gods and goddesses. There is the image of the Princess called *Neang Kong Hing* with huge locks of hair from which she squeezes forth a flood of water in which there are crocodiles that devour the demons preventing Buddha from achieving enlightenment.

Water, unsurprisingly, is at the heart of sex, love and romance and reproduction. When a woman gives birth the Khmer expression is *"Chlong Tonle"* (crossing the river). Art shops display the ubiquitous classic fairy tale image of the young nubile maiden with pert breasts, with or without a see through diaphanous cloth draped invitingly over her top, with the water pot on her shoulder. Another popular image is the maiden and her suitor in a boat on the river, or walking among the rice paddies singing love songs in splendid regalia. (The Khmer culture has thousands of such love songs that have been turned into karaoke CDs and tapes.)

DO join in the karaoke singing when you visit your Khmer friends. Try it - the Khmer love to sing and are delighted if you join in. They will have English songs, usually soppy love songs that you've probably never heard of, B grade muzak - but who cares. So sing along to *"I don't like to sleep alone"* and *"Sha la la la la in the morning"*.

The mighty Mekong and Tonle Sap

The Mekong begins its life in the Thangha Shan Mountains on the Tibetan Plateau and travels southeast through Indochina traversing Myanmar, Laos, Thailand, Cambodia and ultimately to the Mekong Delta in Vietnam. Its total length is 4,200km of which 500km lie in Cambodia. Every year the Mekong floods and brings silt and mud that fertilises the land and forms the basis of this agricultural society. There is also a great abundance of fish.

The Mekong River enters Cambodia from Laos in the north and travels south for a while and then turns west to the place where one of the world's most remarkable natural hydro-logical phenomena is found: a river that changes direction twice a year. At a place called Chatamouk (literally four faces - the four faces of the *stupas* of Angkor) it coalesces for just a kilometre or so with the Tonle Sap River that flows from a lake of the same name. The two rivers then part and go their separate ways to Vietnam, although the Tonle Sap changes name to the Bassac River. This is the meaning of the four faces. This rather stumpy four-faced *stupa* is a central motif in Cambodia.

The Tonle Sap Lake

Tonle Sap means "Great Lake" and is a huge natural water reservoir at the north of which lies the ancient city of Angkor. It is the life-blood of the Cambodian people. The lake system is full of many varieties of fish and edible plants which make up the diet of the Cambodian people. The lake and the Tonle Sap River are also major transport routes for Cambodians travelling throughout the country. Here is how the system works.

When the snows melt in China in spring the Mekong begins to rise. The seasonal Monsoons come on top of this flow throughout China, Laos, and Thailand and the result is that the Mekong becomes a truly mighty river. The Mekong rises rapidly and floods and since it is higher than the waters in the Tonle Sap River the latter reverses direction and the mighty Tonle Sap Lake is replenished with a huge volume of water. During the dry season (from November to April) the Tonle Sap covers an area of about 3,120 sq. km. During the rainy season (from May to December) the lake expands to many times its size to about 10,000 sq. km. occupying up to one sixth of Cambodia. The monsoon rains also deluge Cambodia and the result is a flooded Mekong, a flooded Tonle

Sap lake and often massive flooding everywhere as Cambodia is basically a flat flood plain. In this season fish migrate upstream to spawn.

Then the rains end, the Mekong subsides and the Tonle Sap River changes direction once more and travels south to the Mekong Delta. Thus the Tonle Sap is the only river that changes direction twice every year. Often political commentators make analogies with the river reversing and the eternal reversing machinations of Khmer politics.

Now you understand why the traditional Khmer house is on stilts and why you see dams, or water reservoirs, built ABOVE the surrounding ground level - they are filled by the monsoon rains and then used for irrigation without pumping in the dry season.

Water is the source of two pillars of Cambodian life - rice and fish. Too much water and the rice paddies flood for too high and too long and the rice dies. BUT the other side to this is lots of fish. *"Bad for rice - good for fish"* is a well-known Khmer saying. Rice is sacred to the Khmers as it is for many Asian people. In the western Christian tradition we say "break bread with me", in Cambodia it's "do you want to eat rice with me?" So when invited **DO** eat rice with your friends.

The end of the rainy season in Cambodia brings the great celebration of the "boat races festival" (*Bon Omtup*) in late October or early November, which always happens on the full moon. **DO** try and time your visit to Cambodia to see this festival. Hundreds of beautifully decorated boats and crew race down the Tonle Sap River to the Chatamouk junction with the Mekong in front of the Royal Palace. Some boats have a young woman dressed in traditional clothes swaying to the boatman's whistle.

The end of the rainy season is also fish harvest season. If all goes well, plentiful fish harvests fill the peoples stomachs and surplus fish is preserved in earthen pots as *"Prohok"* or fermented fish paste - Cambodian blue vein. Very, very salty and smelling strongly like rotten fish, restaurants call it Khmer cheese. Khmers and acclimatised foreigners love it. So **DO** sample it, especially in the classic Khmer dish of *"Amok"* which is tasty fish curry.

ANGKOR

Cambodia

It is not possible to write about Cambodia without considering Angkor. This is one of the Seven Wonders of the World, and is the largest Vedic monument and the largest religious building complex in the world. The main temples are not bigger individually than St. Peter's but the whole complex certainly is. So **DO** visit. Angkor is the nation's most powerful symbol representing the zenith of the "golden age" for Cambodian civilisation, the period from the ninth to the fourteenth centuries when the Khmer Empire was the most powerful and successful state and culture in Southeast Asia. This powerful symbol is on the Khmer flag and is a source of great pride to the Khmer. Remember though that Angkor is the largest and grandest of a great number of ancient temples in Cambodia and neighbouring Thailand as well as Myanmar. So Cambodia is an archaeologists dream and a must see.

The experience you have at Angkor will depend on you. It is so vast and there are so many temples that it is impossible to see it all. There are two ways of experiencing it. One is to follow the local guides and your own sensitivities and whims and take it as it comes. The other is to study beforehand and plan your trip making sure you don't miss anything of interest. The approach you take is up to you.

Angkor is truly great, wonderful and awe inspiring and beyond words. However there are a few useful tips to remember.

• **DO** consider taking a trip by boat either to or from Phnom Penh to Siem Reap. The Angkor civilisation was based on water and the bounty of the Tonle Sap. So do go and see the lake - it is a wonderful ride. **DO** plan your trip though. If you go in the peak of the wet season the water is high and the current may be racing downstream so fast that the boat may take longer going against the current while the trip down to Phnom Penh will be one hour shorter. Be careful in the peak of the dry season as the river depth is low, the speed slow, and the changes of boat necessary.

• **DO** treat the temples with respect and protect them. Cambodians are understandably very proud of Angkor.

• The Government sees tourism as the major opportunity for

economic growth and foreign money and markets Angkor strongly. The result is huge numbers of tourists especially in the peak season of November to February. Consider coming in the wet season when there are fewer tourists and the temples rise out of the wet steamy jungle. Also note that Khmer New Year is not a good time to visit as the crowds peak.

• **DO** remember that there are many temples located throughout Cambodia including some not far from Phnom Penh city. In fact there are so many sites it is hard to list them all.

• **DO** know that there are many guidebooks and photographic books available.

• **DO** make use of local taxis and motordops (i.e. motorbike taxis - these are older less expensive bikes which are easily recognised by the driver wearing an unofficial uniform of a baseball cap) that are readily available and are a convenient form of travel to get around the site. Usually two passengers is the limit at double the fare for a single. So you may as well take two motor taxis, unless you are a couple and the woman wishes to feel more secure having her partner close.

• **DO** expect to be impressed with the linguistic abilities of the local tour guides who have excellent language skills in English, French and other languages and who have a good knowledge of the history and temples. They are eager to tell you all.

• **DO** keep your pass on you at all times, as you will have to show it at almost all temples. Passes cost US$20 for one day and require a photograph. Passes for two or three days cost US$40. You can come and go freely from the site while your pass is valid as it is date stamped. You cannot extend your pass and if you lose it there is no pity - buy another.

• **DON'T** forget the park opens at 6 a.m. and closes at 6 p.m. so you can't stay out there at night under the moonlight.

• There is little spiritual ambience at the main Angkor complex and no place to sit and meditate or worship quietly. Yet you will find wonderful oases of silence and beauty off the beaten track. The Khmers visit the Angkor site in large numbers to see it and take photographs. Unlike the Shwedagon Pagoda in Yangon, Myanmar which is a truly functioning pagoda at which the Burmese come to meditate, there is no spiritual feeling at Angkor today - certainly not when surrounded by many thousands of tourists.

• **DON'T** expect bijou restaurants at the site. You will have to go into Siem Reap if you want a good meal.

• **DO** bring your walking shoes as there are many, many steps.

• Also **DO** take water and cameras and portable videos. Professional film crews or those with bigger cameras will need to buy passes for these.

Enjoy - Angkor is an experience of a lifetime.

HISTORY

Cambodia

Cambodia is a history lovers dream. Its history is long, complex, full of intrigue, invasions and wars, glorious victories and devastating savage defeats, kings and concubines, treachery and loss of territory, diverging worldviews, ferocious arguments amongst scholars and intellectuals, continuing political machinations, global superpower rivalries and power games. So if you want to understand it you have your work cut out. This book does not present a critique of the history, as it is too complex. But it does give you a kaleidoscopic view so **do plunge in**.

Since the history is so complicated and so fractious and because of the massive dislocations caused by the KR regime (especially the low literacy levels and poor education standards) the Khmers themselves are divided and lacking knowledge about their own culture and history. There are many people working to help Khmers learn their own history - sometimes with mixed results.

Here is a question for you from a knock-off Trivial Pursuits game developed by a local NGO trying to help rebuild the society: What date was the birth of democracy in the Kingdom of Cambodia? Answer Sept. 1, 1946. Another question is: What year was democracy implemented for the first time in the Kingdom of Cambodia? Answer: 1947.

So **DON'T** expect to be able to get clear, thorough analyses of the history except from a small, educated group that have the analytical and conceptual skills as well as the ability to converse with you in English or French. You are much more likely to receive silence or a smile or "I'm not sure" or "I don't know" if you ask many pointed questions.

Wars and Peace, Peace and Wars

- Victory over the Thais (Siem Reap, the Province where Angkor Wat is located means literally "Thai Defeated".)

- Victory over the French (1952 - 1953, Cambodia obtained complete independence from France.)

- Victory over the Americans (i.e. the defeat by the KR in April 1975 of General Lon Nol, the pro-USA military leader installed by the US in a coup in 1970.)

- Victory over the Khmer Rouge, when Vietnamese backed forces led by Hun Sen, Heng Samrin, Pen Sovan and Chea Sim captured Phnom Penh on January 7th 1979.

- Victory over the Vietnamese (a fixation of the Khmer People.)

Here is an abbreviated list of the main periods and events just to orient you. Even though it is a summary it may seem exhausting. But if you want to understand Cambodia **DO** understand that power and politics is central to the story.

- **Funan Empire**, the earliest recorded state in the region, which was centred on the Mekong delta.

- **550 - 650 AD**, several Khmer states around the Tonle Sap (the great lake in NW Cambodia) rose and replaced Funan. The Khmer influence extended into present day Lao PDR and Thailand.

- **802 - 805 AD**, reign of Jayavarman II, the first Khmer empire-builder.

- **9th - 13th centuries**, the golden age of the Khmer Empire.

- **1432**, the abandonment of Angkor.

- **1561 - 1618**, Capital moved to Longvek, 60 km north of Phnom Penh, ruled by about 15 kings.

- **1618 - 1775**, Udong, just north of Phnom Penh, was occupied as the royal capital.

- **1861**, power moved to Phnom Penh.

- **19th century**, French occupation.

- **1863**, treaty signed with the French.

- **1884**, French imposed a treaty limiting the king's power, abolished slavery and established a colonial bureaucracy.

- **1941**, French Governor General appointed Prince Sihanouk to the throne to become His Majesty Norodom Sihanouk, King of Cambodia.

- **1944**, Thailand occupied the Provinces of Battambang and Siem Reap in North West Cambodia.

- **1945**, (March) King Sihanouk proclaimed independence from France.

- **1946**, French re-established themselves.

- **1947**, King Sihanouk working with the French regained control of and Siem Reap from the Thais. Deep animosity continues to today between Thailand and Cambodia over ownership of Angkor.

- **1952 - 1953**, Cambodia obtained complete independence from France.

- **1952**, France formerly gave what is now South Vietnam, including Prey Nokor (now called Ho Chi Minh city), to North Vietnam. Khmer bitterly resent this loss of land they claim as their own.

- **1955 (April)**, Sihanouk abdicated the throne in favour of his father, His Majesty Norodom Suramarit and founded the Popular Socialist Community Party or Sangkum Reas Niyum and became Prime Minister after this party won the election in 1955. Sihanouk named himself Chief of State and Head of Government. He was, and still is, known by his people as the "Father of the Nation".

- **1954 - 1970**, Sihanouk dominated Cambodian politics, ruling in a highly authoritarian and centralised government. Some say Hun Sen today is just following the only system of Government that Cambodians have known.

- **1970 March 22**, while on an official visit to the USSR, Sihanouk was overthrown in a military *coup d'etat* by General Lon Nol, the pro-USA military leader.

- **1970 October**, Lon Nol proclaimed the Khmer Republic and abolished the monarchy. Sihanouk lived in exile in Beijing and allied himself with the KR who were also opposed to the republican, Lon Nol.

- **1973**, the USA launched massive aerial bombings throughout the country killing up to 150,000 innocent people and destroying the country's infrastructure. Some historians suggest this is what drove the Cambodian people into the arms of the KR.

- **April 17, 1975**, the KR took Phnom Penh and Democratic Kampuchea was established. Cambodia's darkest period descended upon the country as the world's largest decentralisation programme was implemented as Phnom Penh was cleared of all its residents. Over the next four years between one and three million people died from torture, overwork or starvation. During the KR time the traditional (and strongly entrenched and continuing) antipathy for the Vietnamese re-emerged and the KR attacked Vietnamese forces along the border. In late December 1978, the Vietnamese had had enough and attacked the KR.

- **January 1979**, Phnom Penh fell to the Vietnamese, Pol Pot and his followers fled for the jungles along the Thai border, continued to receive political and military support from China and maintained a guerrilla war against the occupying forces.

- **1979**, the Vietnamese installed the PRC (People's Revolutionary Council) led by ex KR commanders Heng Samrin, Chea Sim and Hun Sen. Hun Sen at 32 years of age became the world's youngest foreign minister and later served for a short time as Prime Minister. Now more than 20 years later he and his CPP (Cambodian People's Party – the communist party) remain as the dominant political force in Cambodia today. Hun Sen is currently Prime Minister and is often referred to as the "Strongman of Cambodia".

- **1979 - 1992**, other groups opposed to the PRC "Vietnamese puppets" were headed up by Sihanouk. In 1982, following pressure from ASEAN, these disparate groups united in their opposition to the Vietnamese controlled government. Sihanouk became president of this alliance and the government in exile held the UN seat, and was dominated by the KR. By 1987, there were over 250,000 Cambodian refugees in Thai border camps. The superpowers supported various groups - the USA supported the government in exile to "punish" Vietnam.

- **September 1989**, the Vietnamese withdrew from Cambodia leaving four competing factions seeking control of the country.

- **April 1989**, the SOC (State of Cambodia) was established by the CPP but no consideration was given to power sharing with the other factions. Reconciliation of the major factions is still the major political issue governing modern day Cambodian life.

- **1989**, the French Government convened the Paris International Conference on Cambodia which included 20 nations, the four factions and the UN Secretary-General. A force named UNTAC (United Nations Transitional Authority of Cambodia) was formed.

- **March 1992**, 21,000 UNTAC staff from 40 nations arrived in Cambodia, bringing US$2 billion into the country. UNTAC was charged with overseeing the May 1993 elections, disarming military factions in the country and repatriating hundreds of thousands of refugees from the Thai border camps.

- **1993**, the Royal Government of Cambodia was formed by a power sharing relationship brokered by Sihanouk whereby Hun Sen became second Prime Minister and Prince Norodom Ranariddh (Sihanouk's son) the leader of FUNCINPEC (the royalist party which won the majority of votes) was first Prime Minister. The KR were not included in this Government and continued to wage a guerrilla war. The power sharing relationship between the CPP and FUNCINPEC was very fractious and later disintegrated.

- **September 24, 1993**, Sihanouk was sworn in as His Majesty Preah Bat Samdech Preah Norodom Sihanouk Varman, King of Cambodia.

- **July 1997**, Hun Sen staged a bloody coup and took power. Prince Ranariddh was exiled in Thailand. The international community's funds flowing into Cambodia were restricted and many development projects stalled due to the uncertainties. The coup came on top of the Asian economic crisis and once again Cambodia descended into darkness. Economically the country was set back severely for a few years. Negotiations to patch up political relationships began once again within the country under external pressure.

- **April 1998**, Pol Pot the supreme leader of the KR died of dubious causes in the northern jungles of Cambodia bordering Thailand and was cremated quickly before any forensic examination could be completed. Foreign journalists witnessed and photographed the corpse and cremation and broadcast the news internationally. The cause of Pol Pot's death remains a mystery, as was most of his life. But he *was* dead.

- **July 1998**, the second democratically convened elections were held. Hun Sen won but not with the two-thirds majority needed for the CPP to rule alone. There were calls of poll fraud and after an extended bloody period, which was covered by the international media, without a clearly defined leader and parliament King Sihanouk convened a summit in Siem Reap to resolve the differences between Hun Sen and Ranariddh. Key opposition leader Sam Rainsy who had been the FUNCINPEC Finance Minister in the previous Royal Government was excluded from the final agreement. Hun Sen was formally appointed Prime Minister in November 1998 and at the same time, long time rival Prince Ranariddh became the National Assembly Chairperson. A new Chamber of Government – the Senate – was formed and headed by CPP President Chea Sim. There were charges that the Senate was unnecessary and was just a sinecure for the CPP President. This resolved a deadlock and a power sharing agreement was signed, although tensions remain.

- **Late 1998**, the Khmer Rouge was weakened by the defection of two of its remaining hard liners, Khieu Samphan and Noun Chea. They said they wanted to "live as normal citizens" and were "very sorry" for the suffering wrought by the ultra-leftist agrarian revolution. KR Foreign Minister Ieng Sary had previously received a pardon from the King after written requests co-signed by Ranariddh and Hun Sen.

• **July 2003**. Following the July election conflict between Cambodia's three main political parties resulted in a delay of one year before the formation of a government. International Development agencies and all donors (with one or two exceptions) waited for the formation of a constitutionally mandated government before signing agreements for new programmes of assistance. China signed agreements worth $600 million in April 2004 with the non-constitutionally mandated Government. This large amount, which far exceeds the aid of most other donors, underscores the great importance of China to Cambodia in political and economic terms. Yet despite political tensions between the different political parties the Government is outward looking and making an effort to connect Cambodia with international bodies (especially ASEAN) and regional forums.

Political intrigue continues and is the subject of much debate to this day. The KR trial with UN involvement remains an ongoing circus. So **DO** expect to hear people arguing their case. Foreign experts can be deeply divided and opinionated – sometimes more than the Khmers. It is certain that politics have been, and will continue to be, central to Cambodia's reconstruction. May you live in interesting times! The position you take is after all – up to you.

CONSEQUENCES
OF THE WARS
AND KHMER ROUGE

Cambodia

The human resource deficit - illiteracy and poor education - especially women

The consequence of the "killing fields" of the KR is a lack of people with professional skills. This leads to severe problems of illiteracy, innumeracy and in general very low levels of even basic education. There are lots of jobs for teachers and trainers. The education deficit often leads to massive communication problems. So **DON'T** expect people to understand you or to be able to analyse and plan as you are used to back home. **DO** try and be patient and "say what you mean and mean what you say". **DON'T** expect people to be able to "read between the lines" - be clear and explicit in your requests.

Law, lawlessness, impunity for the rich and powerful - beware of gangsters and the "Bong Thom" - moneyed toughs

Khmer culture can be understood in terms of the powerful doing whatever they want and the powerless having to cop it. Laws are used by the rich and powerful to protect themselves and their assets. **DO** understand that the powerful have impunity so don't get into fights with their bodyguards or the police.

Many people feel that impunity and the weak judiciary system are two fundamental issues limiting Cambodia's development. We all agree it's a biggy - but what to do.? This is the 640 million dollar per year foreign aid question. In practical terms the major effects of this impunity are:

- A corrupt court system - where the rich and powerful walk free and the innocent are damned. If caught by police for whatever reason **DO** expect to pay a bribe.
- The children of high ranking officials - these teenage gangs are a major worry as their members are used to being able to do what they want and have guns and lots and lots and lots of money. **DON'T** pick a fight if some very well heeled kid with body-guards orders you off *his* table in a restaurant or away from *his* parking site.

Corruption

Now here is a big topic - the "C" word which is the subject of endless debates and forums. Some people will say "my God I had to provide a lot of oil to get that deal going", whereas others will say "by comparison with Country X, Cambodia is really quite good and corruption is not so bad" - it is up to you. It is true that salaries (official salaries that is) are very low - $20 - $40 per month for a teacher or doctor in the public service. Yet people pay thousands for government jobs. Why do you think this is so?

Corruption is so endemic that recent surveys indicate that at least 90 percent of Cambodians consider it normal. Corruption plagues all levels of the military, religious and political sectors and is standard operating procedure. When my wife went to register our car she had to pay more than the officially listed price so she accused the person at the motor registry of being corrupt, to which he responded, "look, my director can get a lot of money from just one big transaction so I have to charge everybody who comes to register a smaller amount to make an equivalent amount - this is not corruption". Corruption in the public sector is most prevalent and is perceived as a natural entitlement - a compensation for all the suffering during the Pol Pot regime and the difficulties of the 1980's when the US led an embargo against the country.

The good news for those wanting a long sojourn is that visas can be extended by a simple cash transaction so that anybody (almost) can stay in Cambodia as long as he/she wants by doing a deal with an official at the visa office (although the process is much facilitated if you deal with the policeman outside carrying bunches of passports in his pocket.) This fact has not gone unnoticed by certain questionable individuals. Traffic offences too can be simply dealt with.

Fear and fragmented society - loss of trust and social bonds

Tragically, the Khmer people are deeply traumatised by the past and can become terrified by a minor threat that would not cause you to be concerned. This is why Cambodians are keen to go out together to eat and socialise. They need to feel safe and to have friends. Powerful people can easily remind the population of the dire consequences of not doing what they are told. Here is an example. In the period leading up to recent elections, villagers were asked to come and drink water with a bullet in it. The implication is clear "vote the right way or get the bullet."

If you are out with your Khmer friends or having a party **DO** take note that while some people stay out late most Khmers like to go to a party early and then go home early and lock up. So your party should start earlier than you would in the west - say 5:30 or 6 p.m. not 8:00 p.m., if you want Khmers, especially young women, to attend.

DO recognise that trauma and fear exists and don't be surprised by some peoples' cautiousness, conservatism, lack of trust, lack of initiative and readiness to charge ahead and throw care to the wind. Cambodian's are not ready to say "what the heck"!

Here is an example. I was driving with my Khmer wife to the coastal resort area of Kampot which is the main town before you get to the sea at Kep. We had not been there before and there were no traffic signs. When we arrived in the market of Kampot town I pulled up next to some motorbike taxis and said to my wife "ask them the way to Kep". She loudly and angrily shouted *"don't stop - keep going".* She later stopped at some shops and then started chatting with some women vendors. Once she felt safe and was sure that the women would not lie, only then did she ask the way. She explained *"we can't trust anyone - maybe the motorbike taxi drivers will lie to us and then send us the wrong way so that they can follow and rob or*

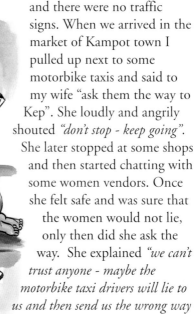

kill us". My wife had spent the KR time as a child in Kampot province.

Older people lament the loss of cultural values. Again and again you will hear how in the past before the KR, people helped their neighbours but now, friends will steal from friends. People used to trade favours but with the loss of family structures and so much migration and social dislocation there is a loss of trust.

DON'T be surprised and upset at the numerous requests you will get for money. It can hurt when someone you thought was a friend asks for an amount which is far beyond your expectations of reasonable. **DO** try not to show that you are upset. Smile and say "I am sorry I don't have".

So **DON'T** be naive and trusting of all people. Some poor souls have become very twisted and hardened by all the trauma of the past. A friendly smile may be a crocodile smile - hang on to your valuables and passports especially when travelling in local taxis across borders. Many people are ripped off.

Repressed anger that can erupt suddenly. - DO BEWARE OF VIOLENT MOBS

The Khmer will say they are a gentle people (unlike the Vietnamese according to the Khmer) - but if this were so where did all the violence of the past come from? In reality despite the smiling there is an undercurrent of anger and violence, which erupts sometimes - luckily not too often. This can be terrifying and can lead to horrible, ugly and tragic events. Thieves (suspected or real) may be killed by mobs in the street. **DO** be very careful if you find yourself nearby, or worse still, in the middle of a violent crowd.

Shattered infrastructure

The story goes that Pol Pot got angry with his electrical engineer and had him killed - so no more repairs of the generator = darkness. The madness of the KR time trashed and ransacked Phnom Penh, the most beautiful capital of the orient (Phnom Penh was the capital of the French colony of Indochine that included Vietnam, Cambodia and Laos and was considered more beautiful than Bangkok in the 60's) and everything else in the country. Now with new found peace, the Cambodian Government backed by the international community and new private investment, is flat out renovating and rebuilding. So **DO** expect lots of challenges, such as:
- Atrocious roads, with huge holes and/or whole sections missing.
- Road repairs without adequate signs.
- Gaping holes in highways with no warnings or markings.
- Piles of dirt and gravel dumped in the middle of roads.
- Sudden road repairs and street closures.
- Interrupted electricity and phone services.
- Flooding drains in heavy rains.

The upside is that when the road construction binge is over, visiting Cambodia will be a cinch.

SAFETY TIP: A branch stuck in the middle of the road indicates a deep hole - beware!

Relearning their own roots and culture

DO understand that there is a great resurgence and interest in some quarters in reviving Khmer culture. Much needs to be done and you can help. It is fascinating to work with Khmer friends to explore their rich heritage of stories, songs and legends and to rediscover the meaning and purpose of their religious beliefs. At the best of times, many people carry out rituals without truly understanding why. Couple that with the cultural revolution of the KR and there are some serious knowledge gaps.

There are organisations and many voluntary groups regenerating and promoting the arts. **DO** support them by going to traditional concerts and dances. These can be most enjoyable events, much richer in value than a nightclub or watching TV in your hotel. **DON'T** stay in your hotel room watching the BBC or CNN. It will be there when you get home.

DO check the what's on section of the English and French language press (the French are the great patrons of culture) and make the effort to partake. Otherwise you may join the ranks of the tourists who say *"God, there's not much to see in Phnom Penh."* There is but you should look around.

Here are some tips and places to check out in Phnom Penh:
- The markets.
- The French Cultural Centre.
- The National Dance Institute.
- The art shops and galleries on street 178 near the University of Fine Arts.
- The magic circus.
- Performances in the big hotels.
- Pagoda festivals.

Hostility towards their neighbours, Thailand and Vietnam

Despite Nixon's secret war and all the bombing and evil foreign policies of the west and the past French colonisation, the Khmers bear no animosity to westerners, although they may not like the French as much (as they sometimes link aid money to promoting the French language which is much less popular now than English). In fact the Khmer are eager to embrace America's materialism and wealth and emulate it. Western embassies have to fight off the crowds of Khmers who queue daily to apply for visas to go to the U.S., Australia, the U.K. and so on.

However it is a different story with the countries neighbouring Cambodia. As a result of the history of wars, land grabbing and territory loss to their neighbours, the Khmer bear great antipathy for the Thais and Vietnamese although the latter are the most vilified. The Khmer really hate the Vietnamese. It is a tragic fixation of the Khmer people, so do be aware of it. If you have a Vietnamese wife or girl friend it may be best to say she is Chinese. **DON'T** be surprised if you hear very disparaging comments about the Thais and most especially the Vietnamese. **DO** be especially sensitive on this issue - don't make enemies by praising Thailand or Vietnam and at the same time criticising Cambodia in the presence of your Khmer colleagues or friends.

DON'T make comparisons between Cambodia and its neighbours. Especially **DON'T** praise the neighbours in front of your Khmer friends. Here is a case from foot in the mouth yours truly who after visiting Thailand managed to really offend his Khmer wife by going on and on and on about how great Thailand was in comparison with Cambodia (**DO** as I say not as I did). *"Wow, I really loved Thailand, so much better than Cambodia. Cleaner, more modern, the people are polite and the hotels know how to deliver service and are cheaper. There are restaurants that understand how to do food for farangs. There are banks where I can use my*

Australian ATM, I loved it". This is not the way to make a favourable impression.

Men **DO** take note, if you are in bar and thinking of taking some girl home, there are two distinct groups - Khmer and Vietnamese. If you go with a Vietnamese girl one night and go back a second night and try and mix with the Khmer girls you may be in the doghouse.

Occasionally this antipathy and resentment of their neighbours erupts. Not so long ago a group of Thai tourists in Siem Reap threw candies to street children and then laughed and took photos as the children fought over them. There was a riot. The tourists had to be escorted back to Thailand by the police. Cambodians said this incident reminded them of an ancient tale of trickery by the Thai army. The story goes that the Thais had wanted to conquer Angkor but were hindered by thick thorn bushes. They threw gold coins into the bushes and the Khmer cut down the bushes to get at the coins thus allowing the Thai army to defeat them. So **DON'T** throw coins or candies and laugh and film children fighting over them.

Khmers are acutely sensitive of their cultural heritage. There is an ongoing complaint with a Thai airline that flies directly from Bangkok to Angkor. The airline has painted a huge picture of Angkor Wat on the fuselage of its aircraft as an obvious marketing tool. However, Cambodian Government officials have complained that it is an attempt by the Thais to claim Angkor as their own. Another example was recent official concern at the selling of traditional ox carts to Thailand. The Khmer authorities wanted to ban the practice as they were resentful of the Thais taking their cultural icons.

So if you like to watch kick boxing (called *"pro dahl"*) with your Khmer friends **DON'T** call it Thai Boxing - it is ancient Khmer boxing and can be seen on the bas reliefs at Angkor.

Khmer Boxing

Marlboro Country - a cowboy country

Cambodia can be a wild and crazy place - lawless, uncontrolled, raw and exciting. It's all here and readily available - sex, drugs and rock and roll. Forget traffic rules - no helmet, no licence, who cares?

DO be aware that the fun wild side means that risks are higher. **DO** take care as you are more on your own. You may not find an ambulance and a hospital when you need one.

Some people find this wild side exciting, fun and liberating while others find it very threatening. **It's up to you.** For those who are tired of suburbia and all the rules of the west, look no further. Take note however, that Cambodia is changing fast and more rules are coming.

Materialism and social status

DO expect to see lots of tinsel and glitz and people showing off their wealth. Khmers can look like Christmas trees without the flashing lights once they wear all their gold jewellery. Children are dressed up in wonderful Shirley Temple outfits with bells, bows and ribbons and of course the mandatory gold necklaces, earrings and anklets. You may well ask: "Do they dig holes in their gardens at midnight to 'bank' their cash and jewels?" The answer is 'no' they are put in boxes and locked up or put under the mattress. People especially love mobile phones with flashing keyboards and TV games...

DO get your cameras ready. **DO** expect to be surprised to see houses that look like "wedding cakes" - painted in pastel or bright colours with lovely trim and shiny stainless steel railings. Often you will see wall hangings with the Buddha adorned with flashing lights and tinsel. Accessories on

cars are also a great hit - lots and lots of extra lights around number plates and windows. The ultimate is of course a bunch of plastic bananas and some cuddly stuffed toy dog on the back windshield with a policeman's cap. I remember hearing a car that played the theme from the movie
"Lambada" when it indicated a turn.

The great interest in gold jewellery is partly a consequence of the weak banking system that is just now being put into some form of regulatory framework. The KR destroyed the banks and since then there have been cases of depositors being cheated and losing their savings so Cambodians don't trust banks. **DON'T** be surprised to see people wearing large chunks of gold - it is their status symbol and bank account all in one.

Sometimes the Khmers appear very opportunistic and money hungry, which can be ugly and create a bad feeling. But when you have so little, isn't this to be expected? You may find yourself being prevailed upon to help with someone's medical bills. Unfortunately because of the past (and some would argue continuing feudal system) the Khmers are used to handouts from their patrons - be it the King or Prime Minister or senior government official. So they have a tendency not to have to take charge of their own lives but to ask for help from some more powerful person. Don't be surprised if that more powerful person is you!

A young society - the post war baby boom

Cambodia's population is a young one. The 1997 census found that 50 percent of the population was under 20 years. It is just like the 60s were in the west - a population boom. **DO** expect to see large numbers of young people hanging out in parks and recreation areas. This young society means that dating and social dalliances are the predominant concern of a sizable chunk of the population. Couple this with the loss of cultural traditions, the death of many older people (especially teachers and monks who are the repositories of

wisdom and knowledge), a great migration to the cities for work and opportunities, insufficient jobs for all the newcomers of employment age and HIV/AIDS, and we have what is called by the development people **"the emerging youth problem"**.

Lack of sophistication - rough behaviour

Although the Khmer see themselves as polite, modest, soft and not assertive they can sometimes seem quite rough to the foreigner. For example, Khmers - especially youths don't queue at banks, shops, offices, etc. **DON'T** get upset (or angry) if you are waiting patiently in line and somebody walks to the top of the queue. It's very French.

Khmers can also be very curious so **DON'T** be surprised if everyone near you in the photo shop gathers round and looks at the pictures that you've just collected and are viewing for the first time. **DON'T** be put off by someone gently working their long finger nail up their nose to pick some annoying buggy which will be wiped clean on the nearest object. **DON'T** be shy to clear your throat and cough and spit up the sputum - why keep a dirty hanky in your pocket?

RELIGION

Cambodia

Buddhism is the dominant and official state religion

Theravada or Hinayana Buddhism is the basic force that shapes social and moral development in the country. Hinduism was the first recorded religion in Cambodia with many of the Angkor monuments belonging to this period. King Jayavarman VII introduced Buddhism into Cambodia in the 12th Century. Before the KR regime there were about 40,000 to 50,000 monks. Pol Pot and the KR regarded them as parasites and forced them into labour camps. Many *wats* were desecrated and their monks killed. Other religions were also persecuted. As a result of the purging of religious personages and the destruction of sacred books, Buddhism in Cambodia today is very impoverished - with much work ahead to rebuild itself. Friendly Buddhist countries and foreign monks are helping in this task of rebuilding the nation's religion.

Buddhism is recognised as the state religion under the Constitution. Nation, Religion, King is the Nation's motto, the three pillars of the Royal Kingdom of Cambodia. Pagodas, temples or *wats* as they are known locally, are being rebuilt and reclaiming their place at the centre of the community, offering not only a place for worship but a whole range of social welfare services.

DO know that as in any other Buddhist or Hindu country, Thursday is the day of religious observance. **DO** understand that devout Buddhists will fast and go to a pagoda. Families will often make offerings of fruit, flowers and water at the shrines in their houses.

What to do when visiting the *wat*

DO make an effort to visit the *wats*. It is fascinating to see the old ruins being restored and to see the wide variety of ceiling and

wall decoration. In the countryside there are some magnificent ancient structures that are once more the centre of village life. Traditionally, *wats* were places of learning and to reassume that role are being rebuilt throughout the country. Most festivals are linked to Buddhism (*see* Festivals and Holidays). Today there is a great interest on the part of many Khmers to rebuild their *wats* so fundraising is common. One especially popular way is the *kathen* celebration in which a family or person will hold a celebratory dinner and invite a large number of paying guests. The money collected is then taken to a poor pagoda. These *kathen* celebrations are much loved and happen after the Pchum Ben festival (which honours ones ancestors) near the end of the rainy season. The *kathen* are very colourful and happy events - so **DO** go if invited.

DO take off your hat and shoes and **DO** wear a white shirt or blouse when you visit a pagoda. Also make sure to take off your shoes when offering something to a monk. Women may wear other coloured tops if they also wear a plain white sash (e.g. scarf) across their shoulder. Traditionally the sash goes from the left shoulder to the right waist.

Don't sit higher than a monk

When sitting near a monk it is important to bow and not to sit (for example, on a chair) higher than a monk. At pagodas people will sit on the floor. Monks will be seated in a special place sometimes on a raised platform. At other times when the monks are sitting on the floor do follow your Khmer friends lead and you will not have any problem.

DON'T touch a monk if you are a woman, even to shake hands. When a woman wishes to give gifts or alms to a monk, one way is to offer them on a tray so that the monk can collect them later - in this way the monk will avoid touching a female body. As in Thailand, the formal procedure is that the monk sets a cloth on a table or the ground, the lady places her gift on the cloth, the monk steps forward and removes the cloth and gift.

Minority religious groups - the Chinese, Cham Moslems and Vietnamese

Today Cambodia is unusually religiously homogeneous as about 90 percent of Khmers are Buddhist - partially a consequence of the KR attacks against the Cham (Islamic), Vietnamese and Chinese minorities. Yet there are other significant religions including: Chinese religions, Cham Moslems, Indigenous Tribal People's religions and Vietnamese Christians. **DO** your bit to promote religious tolerance by treating all these faiths with due respect.

Chinese religions include Confucianism, Taoism or Chinese Mahayana Buddhism. The Khmer have a dual relationship with the Chinese - on one hand admiring and envying their light skin and intelligence and wealth and financial skill; and on the other resenting or despising these same qualities. Many Khmer homes will have a Chinese shrine. **DON'T** be surprised by the Chinese shrines in offices, shops and homes. Khmers seem to like to have a bet both ways just to be sure.

Although the Chams were persecuted by the KR, there are still about 200,000 living in Cambodia. Their form of Islam is considered moderate. There are several mosques close to Phnom Penh and Cham communities along the Mekong and Tonle Sap Rivers.

Indigenous tribal people are mostly animists or spirit worshippers. They live in some of the more remote and mountainous regions in the North East. There are good spirits and bad spirits and spirit men in the villages communicate with them especially in times of illness.

There are also small numbers of Christians. Close to the capital, churches can be seen amongst the Vietnamese community in particular.

THE MONARCHY -
NATION, RELIGION, KING

Cambodia

His Majesty Preah Bat Samdech Preah Norodom Sihanouk Varman, former King of Cambodia, is one of the great royal personages of our time who "reigns but does not rule" Cambodia. King Sihanouk's life spans an enormous period of history, that is difficult to adequately review or summarise. His Majesty has lived through French colonisation of Cambodia, World War II, *coup d'etats*, exile and imprisonment and most recently reinstatement as King. The former King is famous for his exceptional energy and human skills as well as his devotion to Cambodia, its people and culture. He has made a great many films and has also composed music and songs. His daughter Bopha Dev is famous as an Apsara Dancer with art shops carrying the classic image of her dancing.

The Khmers are quite divided in their feelings for him so do beware when talking about him. He was, after all the leader of the coalition of forces fighting the Vietnamese controlled communist Government headed by Heng Samrin, Chea Sim and Hun Sen, who today remain leaders of the Cambodian People's Party (CPP), the dominant political force in Cambodia today. The media were not permitted to criticise His Majesty. One of the most critical issues facing the country was the successor to King Sihanouk. Cambodia does not have an hereditary system of royal succession. In a peaceful hand over of power, Sihanouk's son, Prince Sihamoni, was crowned King in October 2004.

Most older people love and respect the old King and he is widely considered the "father of the nation" like a tall tree providing cool shade and protection to his people. The young majority of Cambodians who never lived through the heyday of the Sihanouk era in the 60s, have different feelings. Sihanouk is also considered the grand chess master and power broker of Cambodia, playing a key role in times of national crises. He has forged working governments from warring factions on two important recent occasions. The chess analogy is highly relevant as Hun Sen the "strongman of Cambodia" also loves chess and is occasionally referred to as a "chess master".

In more recent times Sihanouk played a reduced role in public affairs and spoke of his life entering a stage like "the setting of the sun". Many people were concerned for the future of the Monarchy while others feel its passing would be the best thing to happen. For the present, the Monarchy continues under the new King.

HUN SEN AND THE CPP,
THE OKNHA

Cambodia

Hun Sen and the CPP - the current power in Cambodia

It would be an oversight in this book not to consider the critically important current status of Hun Sen, his CPP and the role he plays in Cambodia. In 2005 Prime Minister Hun Sen turned 54. He has publicly spoken of remaining PM for at least another 10 years after which time he hopes (and plans to ensure) that his son Hun Manet (who recently graduated from West Point Military Academy in the US) will succeed him.

Hun Sen is loved by some and loathed by others - yet his near control of the country is without doubt. Hun Sen has joked that now Cambodia has joined ASEAN there are three requirements of membership - speaking English, playing golf and eating durian. The golf requirement is taken seriously. He loves to play at Phnom Penh's new courses so if you are a golfer and the opportunity presents itself **DON'T** be shy to challenge him to a game. He is very protective of Khmer culture and has written numerous songs and poems. Hun Sen is also a warrior who sponsors events like Tai Quan Do and Kick Boxing competitions rather than Khmer traditional dancing.

DO be careful what you say and discuss with your Khmer friends. **DON'T** get into loud arguments criticising Hun Sen with soldiers and police, who are likely to be his loyal supporters - you may have a fist in the face or worse.

The Oknha - Mandarins

The *Oknha* are the rich, powerful elite in Cambodia who give very significant donations to the Government (i.e. the CPP and Hun Sen). Cambodia is their town - they are richer and more powerful than you and they know it. One prominent individual publicly boasted of giving Hun Sen US$1,000,000 after the 1997 coup. The *Oknha* usually do not mix it up at backpacker hotels preferring to dine in the comfort of the larger hotels and casinos that they own. Yet they are recognizable by their fleets of Mercedes and numerous bodyguards in accompanying Toyota Land Cruisers.

One of the *Oknha* for example is the owner of the company that controls Angkor and all its tourist revenues. In the past the *Oknha* were given diplomatic passports, a practice that has now been reigned in somewhat. These few individuals are the real powerbrokers of Cambodia. **DO** be careful not to ask too many probing questions with people you don't know.

LANGUAGE

Cambodia

LANGUAGE: The Dutch of Asia. All those vowels

Khmer is the main language of the people of Cambodia and in some North Eastern areas of Thailand and in the Mekong Delta area of Vietnam. This is a result of the historical fact that the ancient Khmer nation extended into Thailand and what is now South Vietnam, including Saigon. The Khmer speakers in Thailand are called Khmer Surin and those in South Vietnam are called Kampuchea Krom (low land Khmer). Khmer has also influenced "Royal Thai", the formal language of the Thai court. One consequence of the KR regime is that more so than in other languages, there is a great difference between spoken colloquial and written or formal Khmer. This is because many people are illiterate and rely on spoken Khmer only. Couple this with the lack of formal schooling for many people and the result is a spoken language that has many short cuts with local vocabulary and incorrect grammar.

DO know that there are significant differences between the Khmer of the CPP and the Khmer spoken by FUNCINPEC and expatriate Khmers. This is a result of the communist times – for example do you use citizen or comrade to refer to a person? The difference is in the words not just pronouns. This difference in language between different groups of Khmer is sometimes a source of friction.

The Khmer language has a complex alphabet with many more vowels and diphthongs than are found in western languages, some of which are difficult, or impossible for westerners to pronounce. Unlike Thai, Vietnamese and some other languages devolved from similar Sanskrit and Pali roots, the Khmer language does not use tones. While this makes it easier for many westerns to speak, it makes it critically important that the vowel sound is accurately pronounced. **DON'T** despair if your attempts at communicating with the locals are a flop – keep trying.

There are a total of 32 consonants in Khmer consisting of two types, as in Sanskrit - unaspirated, spoken explosively without exhalation of breath, and aspirated which sound softer. Consonants at the ends of words are not pronounced or pronounced very slightly. **DON'T** be frustrated if you can't hear the consonants or can't discriminate between them. Vowels consist of two sorts – long and short. There are a total of 23 Khmer vowels, which taking their long and short versions add up to about 60 vowel sounds including several for which there is no western equivalent.

Since each syllable is clearly either short or long, Khmer has a rhythmic sound to it - some have compared it to a verbal morse code. The length of the vowel sound is important so the length cannot be extended at will (for emphasis for example) as in English.

DON'T just jump in a taxi or on a motorbike and expect that your phrase book based pronunciation efforts will get you to your desired destination - there have been amusing cases (not for the person involved) of people ending up in entirely

the wrong province because of mispronunciation. There are also regional dialects and many street name changes to contend with.

Despite these challenges do try and learn a few words and talk with the people who will really appreciate your efforts.

One important aspect to remember in regard to language is that illiteracy levels are high - the KR killed off all the teachers and burned books - so **DON'T** rely on written directions from a literate friend, especially with rural women as many can't read.

MONEY AND BANKS

Cambodia

A greenback based economy

In Cambodia the greenback is supreme. It is a cash-based economy. This is a consequence of the UN presence here in 1992-93 and tourism. Government regulations allow the free use of foreign currency – especially the American dollar, the Thai Baht, the Vietnamese Dong and now at the Prime Ministers direction the Chinese Yuan. There are regional differences. In the northwest areas near Thailand prices are often stated in restaurants and shops in Baht. Near the Vietnamese areas you will see more Dong. In Phnom Penh and major provincial towns there is no problem changing money but beware that once you are out in rural areas the situation is very different – although dollars are accepted everywhere.

DO expect to use dollars everywhere. **DON'T** waste time and effort changing money when you arrive at the airport or border town. In most restaurants and hotels catering for foreigners all prices are given in dollars. Change of less than a dollar is given in the local currency –

the Reil (about 3,900 to the US$). Use the Reil to pay for tips, motor taxis (called motordops) and street stalls. **DO** expect Cambodia to be more expensive than neighbouring countries where you can use local currency and benefit from the exchange rate.

Travellers cheques are another story – only a few banks and bigger hotels and travel agents catering to the foreign community will accept them. Remember the banking sector here is weak and people do not have bank accounts and cheque books.

Ubiquitous money-changers

There are no problems when changing major foreign currencies especially in Phnom Penh. You will find money changers along the streets in cities, especially near markets. They are easily recognised

by their glass cabinets displaying money. **DO** note that they deal with cash and gold only.

The exchange rate is remarkably stable as the local currency is only used in Cambodia and not traded. It rarely fluctuates much from 3,900 Riel to the US$ but the rate does go down near Cambodian and Chinese New Year when rich and powerful people move large amounts of cash to make some extra profits.

Don't expect a national banking system

As a result of its recent history Cambodia does not have a good banking system. In fact there is no national banking system and you will not find banks outside of the capital city of Phnom Penh - so take sufficient funds with you whenever you travel out of the city. Siem Reap is the exception as it is making great efforts to promote tourism and has two banks where you can cash travellers cheques. By the time this book is published there may also be banking services in Kampong Som - but do check first.

Also do expect banks to close for either a day or half a day immediately before or after official holidays for auditing. This can be a real trap if you need cash. Remember Cambodia has 3 New Years – International, Khmer and Chinese, although the latter is not an official holiday, some banks may close anyway.

Do expect the change at markets

One pleasant fact is that the Khmer shopkeepers are not going to try and keep the change and hassle you to take your change in postage stamps. Once the price is agreed do expect to get your change. If one shop cannot change your big note then they will simply ask the neighbouring shop to help. **DON'T** be worried if they disappear and run out the back - they are going to a moneychanger to get your change. **DO** ask them to give you change in dollars especially if you're giving a big note for a small purchase. They can often oblige.

Warning: damaged torn notes are not accepted - don't use $100 bills

DO watch out for damaged notes and sticky tape - they are not accepted. Damaged local currency however, is OK. This is one of the most infuriating experiences to be had in Cambodia. People think the paper is the money and will absolutely stubbornly refuse to accept even slightly damaged notes. If there is a tiny tear or a hole it is worthless. You will have to wait till you get home or palm it off on someone else. An evening can be disenchanting when you pay for a meal only to have huge arguments over your money being too old or torn. $100 notes are

a special problem as there are counterfeit concerns. Many embassies will not accept $100 bills for payment of visas, etc. Best to avoid them altogether. Curiously, small marks and stamps on notes are OK. They often carry stamped seals or initials.

DO keep your money high and dry and clean and crisp and neat and uncrumpled. Stuffing it into pockets is a no-no. The reality is that the national bank does use damaged US$ notes all the time to pay overseas transactions – as they know they are accepted.

Also **DO** be on the lookout for counterfeit US$10 and $20 notes – these are the new arrivals on the block.

Credit cards - do keep them at your hotel

Credit cards are of limited use in the cash based economy of Cambodia. Yet they are becoming more widely accepted and can be used at certain (not all) banks in Phnom Penh for cash advances and at some hotels, especially those catering to foreign tourists. Some restaurants, travel agents and top of the line medical clinics offering emergency evacuations of personnel from embassies and large corporations also accept them. **DON'T** bother taking the chance that your credit cards may be lost or stolen by keeping them on you. Leave them along with travellers cheques at your hotel. Theft from your hotel room is rare in most cases – although when it does happen little can be done. The risk of you being pick pocketed, or robbed or just plain losing your wallet is greater. As in much of Asia, Cambodia has an aversion to American Express cards because of the fee the latter charges them. So if Amex is all you have, **DO** bring plenty of cash or get a VISA card too.

TRAFFIC – ESPECIALLY
IN PHNOM PENH

Cambodia

"Well he had to turn the bike around to see where he was going," my Khmer wife said of the motorcycle rider who suddenly pulled out from the roadside and did a U-turn in front of me without looking. I couldn't believe it. I had to do an emergency break and throw the bike down to avoid hitting him. Luckily my wife, riding side saddle facing to the left, simply waited till the bike almost stopped and jumped off unharmed. The driver muttered, perhaps defensively, that he wished I had hit him as he could then have got some money as it would have been my fault. I asked *"why couldn't he turn his head around and look before he pulled out?"*

The traffic in Phnom Penh is a major daily wonder and conversation topic. Some people say that when you stop screaming and complaining only then have you adjusted well. Others will say that is the time to leave because you have gone local and lost your balance. Can the traffic be described best as chaos or anarchy? – you judge.

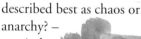

Siem Reap by contrast is a fairly quiet small town with slowly moving traffic, which you will find a welcome change to the conditions you have experienced elsewhere in SE Asia. People drive slowly, give way, and make space for motorcycles. But driving in Phnom Penh presents challenges.

"It's quite simple really darling" said my mother as I was losing the plot and swearing and muttering *"I don't believe he did that"* when I was driving. *"Everybody just goes about their own lives dear and does their own thing - it's quite simple really"* – Zen and the art of driving. When I am in a completely settled and rested state I can almost do it. But we are talking about driving cars, motors, cyclos (rickshaws) and trucks. People drive in the immediate present (thinking no more than a few seconds ahead or reacting as necessary) and only notice things visually when they enter the field of immediate peripheral vision – i.e. two to three meters at most.

DO remember your breathing and expect chaos and to be challenged by vehicles, pedestrians, cows and other animals coming at you from every direction on all sides of the road at all speeds – although luckily usually slowly.

No thinking now - slow speed is the answer - drive at walking pace

Cambodians are now enjoying the use of cars for the first time in decades and have not had the benefit of growing up seeing their parents drive. Cars are flooding into the country and people love to go for a drive – SLOWLY SLOWLY in the MIDDLE OF THE ROAD.

Here is an amusing story.

A woman I met was narrating how she was staying with a Khmer family. Late one afternoon they asked if she wanted to go for a walk. She thought that was a great idea as she wanted to get out for a look see and raced to her room to change into running shoes and walking pants and then went downstairs only to find her Khmer family waiting in their new car. She asked "I thought you said we were going for a walk" and they laughed at her – "no we just say walk but really we mean drive". So drive they did – at walking speed. In fact they drove so SLOWLY and SMOOTHLY that an open flower arrangement in a low flat vase with water located on the arm rest between the two front seats, didn't splash at all.

Some important survival tips:

DO drive on the right – if you can. Officially cars are left hand drive and the rules say drive on the right – but do expect traffic in all directions on all sides of the road. One of the most amazing and amusing sites to video is an intersection at peak hour in Phnom Penh. Drivers just try any available space and will move onto the wrong side of the road on all approaches to the intersection. The result is a massive logjam and traffic backs up for long distances. Naturally now that traffic has stopped the motorbikes just take to the footpaths to cut corners: remember Khmer never walk so pedestrians are no problem. **DON'T** drive through busy intersections at peak hours.

DO drive slowly. The best way to avoid accidents, or to avoid incurring serious damage, injury or loss of life, when crashes do occur is slow (often painfully slowly by Khmer) speed.

DO remember the main road rule – might is right. If you are bigger than the next guy you are in the right, **DO** expect the big guys to ignore you and pull out in front – it is up to you to avoid them.

DO expect to be challenged when making a right hand turn if you are driving a car. The correct position for cars is near the centre of the road or in the left lane if you are on a wider road with multiple lanes for each direction. Motorbikes are required to drive on the right next to the kerb or in the right lane only if there are two or more lanes in each direction. Amazingly, the law (at least as it is understood) is for the car to turn right from near the left of the right lane or from the left hand lane of a wider four lane road. **DON'T** do the western turn whereby you would move to the right of the road to make a right turn, as motorbikes will be annoyed that you are moving into "their" lane. So **DO** indicate and **DO** proceed slowly and let the motorbikes pass - otherwise you'll collect one in your right hand door, attract a crowd of onlookers and have to pay for the damage. Now you understand why motorbikes slam into the right hand side of cars. Here's another rule to see you across an intersection: whoever is in front goes first. The first to the intersection is the first to go–simple!

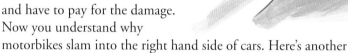

DO watch out for the red and red and blue number plates. These are the military and police cars and they truly are a law unto themselves. The policeman or soldier or official in the fast car who cuts you off, well, he can do anything he wants.

DON'T wait just go. Cross the road step by step. **DON'T** wait till a gap in the traffic appears as it usually never will. Just remember your breathing and keep your eye on the other side of the road – say your prayers and walk slowly step by step. **DON'T** think too much. The traffic will part around you – even cars. My wife will routinely just step out with our baby in a stroller in front of cars and trucks to cross the road.

DON'T use the pedestrian crossing. **DON'T** EVER use these assuming they mean what they do back home. The Khmer have no idea about them and they are worthless at best – usually downright dangerous.

DON'T drive with your lights on in the daytime as this is only for high officials. Remarkably this is the one rule the police really enforce. They consider it an extreme offence if you drive with your lights on, as this is a privilege reserved for the most senior government officials. After the 1998 election senior CPP officials were infuriated when UN vehicles were seen at the front of street demonstrations driving WITH THEIR LIGHTS ON. The situation has eased considerably in recent times as the government has put curbs on officials driving in motorcades as it is an unpopular display of power and force.

DO note that a helmet is advisable. Remember, the traffic is chaos and the medical facilities available for road accident casualties are poor and there may not be an ambulance – so safety first.

Lady passengers – side saddle please and do avoid burns – OUCH. Traditionally lady passengers ride side saddle on motorbikes usually facing left as the hot exhaust pipe is on the right hand side of the bike. Take real care with the exhaust to avoid burns as these can be severe, can become infected and take ages to heal. However if you feel too uncomfortable and unsafe then you can sit normally, straddling the seat – not in a miniskirt or hot pants, ideally. The Khmer will understand your not being used to side saddle, but many women do get used to it.

DO follow police directions for motorcades. Every now and then you will hear the wailing of sirens and notice cars (with their lights on in the daytime) driving down the middle of the road. At these times the traffic police will stop playing cards in the shade of trees or extorting bribes from helpless victims and jump up to stop the traffic. You are expected to pull over. Of course it is hard to be impressed when the last vehicle in the motorcade is a small truck carrying a golf cart. If you see many military policeman with AK47s standing every 50 meters along a road and at corners, it is a sign that the PM or some visiting head of state or very senior person, is going to appear soon. These security details will have ICOM radios and at the appropriate signal will jump out and stop traffic. **DO** obey them.

DO watch out for the Dream Boys – "no brains, no licence, no idea, no problem". Although most people drive slowly – too slowly – there are the young lads on fast motorbikes, like the Honda Dream machine. They love to fly (i.e. drive on the back wheel only down the road) or zigzag in and out of traffic at high speed. They are a danger and frequently crash into innocent people. **DO** watch out as these boys drive like the wind and may be drunk or high on *yaba* (appropriately enough, an illegal drug called *speed*.)

DO note that motorbikes are not permitted on Norodom Boulevard in working hours. Traffic laws are being enforced more and more and certain streets are closed to motorbikes and cyclos. Parking is also restricted on some city streets and police will use this to extract fines – so check out what other cars are doing.

DO know that the police are there for donations. As mentioned earlier, corruption is so endemic in Cambodia that more than 80 percent of Khmers see it as normal and indeed necessary. I was studying Khmer with my neighbour who was a university student. She represents the future of the country and I was speaking with her about the practice of the police in taking bribes. She insisted that this was normal as they had to feed their family. When I persisted she just smiled and it was obvious she wasn't going to change her view. Police buy a posting on profitable intersections and prey on the weak and defenceless. But note they will only stop someone weaker who they can bully without risk, like some obviously poor rural peasant driving into the city. They will not take the risk with the Dream Boys as they may be armed and ready to shoot or be the sons of senior officials. Sometimes police will stop foreigners in cars and demand to see a driving licence – the bribe should not exceed US$10 – usually less will do unless they are very thirsty. Driving licenses are not required to drive motorbikes.

DO note that certain corners are more strictly controlled than others. The most heavily policed intersection is the northeast corner of the Independence Monument. This is near Hun Sen's family house so military and traffic police are always stationed there in some numbers and will stop motorbikes, which are forbidden in working hours (you can drive in lunch time but watch what the locals are doing first). However the other side of the intersection is not patrolled. Usually the best advice if driving a motorbike is to power on through and not stop in the daytime as the police are just after a bribe and are not armed. But be careful not to get stopped further up the road – use a side street. If you do get stopped do smile, don't get angry and abusive and do expect to have to pay and wait a long time and miss your meeting.

However at night **DO** stop at police checkpoints and roadblocks. The police regularly set up roadblocks to check for weapons especially at night and motion you to stop with light batons. There will be armed military police (with an AK47) standing down the road some short distance to catch people who don't stop. **DO** stop as the police usually are after weapons and are particularly focussed on the Khmer people themselves, most especially teenage boys and possible robbers. There are still far too many unregulated guns in Cambodia. Cars are usually waved on through or motioned to go around the checkpoint.

FESTIVALS AND HOLIDAYS

Cambodia

As in neighbouring Thailand there are a great number of holidays which causes great frustration with businesses and organisations trying to follow international practice. Does Cambodia have more holidays than any other country? – you judge. The Government attitude is often expressed as 'since we can't pay our people good salaries we should give them time off – a lot.'

The following is a list of festivals and 24 days of holidays. During national holidays, especially Khmer New Year, the King's Birthday and Boat Racing Festival, the Royal Palace is lit up at night and Phnom Penh's waterfront is very beautiful. Outside of Phnom Penh people will also decorate provincial towns and their homes at these special times. If a holiday falls on a weekend day it is taken on the subsequent Monday. **DO** take note that an official 1-day holiday may become a 4-day weekend as people leave offices early on Friday and don't return till Tuesday. Beware of unexpected bank closings.

Holiday	Fixed or approximate date	Duration
International New Year	January 1	1 day
Victory day – a CPP holiday commemorating the defeat of the KR by Vietnamese backed forces led by Hun Sen. The forced reintroduction of this holiday by Hun Sen was bitterly resisted by other parties, as it also marked the start of 10 years of occupation by the Vietnamese.	January 7	1 day
Chinese New Year – same as Vietnamese Tet Festival. This is not an official Cambodian holiday but is still celebrated by many Khmer and is very important for the Chinese merchant class of Phnom Penh. Many Chinese owned shops and businesses close. The holiday is traditionally celebrated with firecrackers which are banned by the government.	Timing is based on lunar calendar. Holiday may be in January or February	Not an official holiday but last 3 days

Yet you will hear some. Because of the economic power of the Chinese community in Cambodia this holiday is marked by price increases. Shops and houses are decorated with cuttings of a yellow flowering native tree called *Fleur De Tet*. The cuttings will be leafless with flower buds that bloom over the next few days. If the canes have many blossoms this bodes for a profitable year.

Valentines Day. Called "Sweetheart Festival" in Khmer. Popular with younger people.	February 14	Not an official holiday
International Women's Day	March 8	1 day
Khmer New Year. This is the solar New Year and is identical with the Indian (Vedic) New Year and Thai Songkran festival and marks the entry of the sun into the first astrological sign of Aries. *See* extra notes below.	Mid April	3 days
Visak Bochea Day. This is the triple anniversary of the birth, death and enlightenment of Buddha and is celebrated at *wats*.	Late April	1 day

Royal Ploughing Ceremony, which marks the beginning of the rice planting season. The exact day is based on the lunar calendar. The ceremony was reintroduced for the first time in 24 years on May 28th in 1994 and is an ancient festival. It is a time for farmers to prepare the soil for planting. *See* extra notes below.	April or May	1 day
International Labour Day	May 1	1 day
Genocide Day - this is historically a CPP holiday and used to be called a "day of hate" at which people remembered the atrocities of the KR. It is no longer officially celebrated now that the KR have been defeated and reconciled into Khmer society by the government. Yet there will be ceremonies at certain monuments to the dead of the KR - such as the famous "Killing Fields" outside of Phnom Penh and the Tuol Sleng museum.	May 9	Not an official holiday
International Children's Day	June 1	1 day
Queen's Birthday. Birthday of Her Majesty Preah Reach Akka Mohèsey Norodom Monineath Sihanouk	June 18	1 day
Constitution and King's Coronation Day	September 24	1 day
Pchum Ben or Festival of the Ancestors. This is an especially important Buddhist festival commemorating the dead and is the other major festival (beside Khmer New Year) when Khmer MUST visit the *wats*. If people do not then their ancestors will be very unhappy and it brings very bad luck. *See* extra notes below.	Late September or October	3 days
Kathen Tean. While this is not actually a recognised festival, it is an important time of the year for Buddhists and begins after Pchum Ben. It is a wonderful joyful time and coincides with the start of the end of the wet season and happy times ahead. It is very colourful with trucks driving large numbers	October to November	Over 15 days

of people around with Buddhist banners of all colours. *See* extra notes below.

Coronation of King Sihamoni	October 29	1 day
Retired King's Birthday. Birthday of His Majesty Preah Bat Samdech Preah Norodom Sihanouk Varman.	October 31	1 day
Independence Day. Celebrates Cambodia's independence from France in 1953. It is marked by a flame of remembrance at the Independence Monument and an official function at this site. **DO** treat this with great respect and don't approach the flame. There is a ceremonial guard of honour at the flame.	November 9	1 day
Bon Oum Tuk - or the Water Festival or Festival of the Reversing Currents in the Tonle Sap River. This is not a water throwing festival like Khmer New Year. It may extend into the King's birthday and thus October or November may have only 10 working days. People will also take extra days off.	October or November	3 days

December 2. This is an important CPP holiday as it marks the birth of the party but is an unofficial holiday. Nevertheless the CPP may hold its annual congress at this time with streets in Phnom Penh blocked off near the CPP Head Quarters for an entire morning resulting is massive traffic congestion.	December 2	1 day but not an official holiday
International Human Rights Day	December 10	1 day

Not to be outdone in the holiday stakes, the birthday of King Sihamoni will be celebrated in a 3 day holiday equal to that of former King Sihanouk whose birthday will continue to be celebrated. As the country is far too saturated with holidays for the likes of the international community, word is that the Paris Peace Accords holiday will be axed, a proposal that has caused public outcry. Of course, the solution would be to reduce both kings' birthdays to one day, instead of three, and removing International Women's Day, but...

Major festivals, more...

Khmer New Year, same as Songkran

DO know that Khmer New Year is not a wild national water fight. The emphasis is on family visits and games.

This is one of the most important and longest of the holidays and Khmers are under great social obligation to visit the *wats* and to return to their traditional homelands in the provinces to visit family. **DO** visit your Khmer friends house and **DO** note that the exact time of the sun's entry into Aries will be announced. It is important because at that time a new God will descend to earth and the old God departs. People will set up offerings at their door and decorate their houses with fairy lights and candles and watch a special TV programme put on by the government in which computer animation shows the new God descending from the sky to the earth.

People will ensure they are praying in front of their offerings which are sprayed with perfume and jasmine scented water. The Khmer calendar has 12 animals in a 12-year cycle.

Khmer New Year is a very happy time, like the Christmas and New Year period in the west with much merriment and partying. Very few businesses remain open. Like Chinese New Year **DO** expect price hikes so stock up beforehand.

Because of the many traffic accidents and fatalities that occur as motorbikes swerve to avoid being drenched with water, the Government has banned water pistols and asked people not to throw so much water.

New Year is the highlight of the year and is associated with lots of parties, dancing and music in the streets. You will see and feel the energy building up for some weeks beforehand. **DO** join in the parties – you must join in. There used to be fireworks but

these are banned now as the Government is concerned about misuse of guns. Yet sometimes you will hear AK 47 gun shots fired into the air for fun. **DO** remember that what goes up comes down and people have been killed and injured by falling bullets. A man I knew has a hole in the front of his landrover where a bullet landed. So if you hear shots take cover under a heavy branch or solid roof.

Khmers expect New Year bonuses at this time and make plans to travel to distant provinces to visit their homelands and family birthplaces. It is common for Khmer to receive 13 months salary for a year with the 13th pay being made just before New Year. **DO** remember this financial gift.

Traditional Khmer New Year games

During Khmer New Year people usually play traditional games, often in the cool of the evening (it is in the hottest time of year remember). These nights offer some of the best experiences to be had in Cambodia, enjoying the occasion in a genuine way with the Khmer people under the stars. There is much music, dancing and merriment. The games are not just for fun as they provide a means for young single women and men to meet in the guise of family sponsored festivities.

Here is a guide to some of the popular games. **DO** join in.

Card games and gambling

If you are a gambler then Cambodia is for you. The Khmers love to play cards and gamble especially during New Year and Pchum Ben. There are many games which you will have fun learning. Often families will spend hours and hours playing cards with their children. Don't lose your shirt though if you get into some serious games as you may find yourself suddenly with a group of experienced conmen.

Gambling is a hot topic and gets much press and concern. There is a legal casino in Phnom Penh and at least 10 more located on the NW and SW borders with Thailand and the eastern border with Vietnam. The Khmer are not supposedly allowed to gamble in Phnom Penh as the powers that be are afraid that their families will be the targets of kidnapping for ransom payments when gamblers lose big. This is a real and valid fear as kidnappings peak around major gambling events like world cup soccer competitions and big international fights. There are direct flights from China and Hong Kong bringing in big players to the casinos.

Since they can't go to the casinos the humble village folk bet on the sky and when it will rain, as well as cock fighting, many lotteries and smaller card games.

Le-ak Kansieng (or hide a towel at your back)

People of all ages sit in a mixed circle facing inwards and one person is outside carrying a towel. S/he will walk around the backs of the people and place the towel behind someone. When the towel is placed behind you, you jump up and grab it and try to catch the person sitting on your right and hit them with the towel. They will be racing as fast as they can around the circle back to their seat. Once they sit down then you go around and put the towel on the left side of the next victim. Lot's and lot's of running and screaming.

Boh Ang Kunh (or throwing the seeds of the Ang Kunh tree) - watch your knees

This is a dangerous game for men: beware the girls hit hard. This is how it works. Boys stand at one end and women at the other. Dried *ang kunh* seeds (usually 3 - 5) are placed on the ground by one group in front of them – say the boys. Next the girls throw other seeds to try and hit the target, like *patanque* or French *boules*. If they are successful then put on your knee pads. The girls hold two seeds one facing the other and "tap" you on the knee. There should be a nice little "click" but they hit very hard

and beat the crap out of your knees. **DO** expect to be bruised and very sore the next day.

When the boys win and get a chance to hit the girl's knees, the girls (in long dresses or sarongs) will put one knee forward for you. **DON'T** do as she did to you and retaliate: just a tap is enough.

Boh Choung (or throwing a small pillow - a pillow fight under the stars)

This is a lovely game that allows the sexes to mingle and goes on for hours under the stars. Men at one end, women at the other. One side starts – say the men. One man lobs a small soft pillow at the ladies. If a lady catches it she can then throw it back as hard as she can to hit a man. If successful the ladies can extract a payment which means you must either sing a song or dance while you make your way slowly and gracefully down the corridor between the two ends. Everyone claps and there is lots of laughter and happiness. Then the game starts over again.

Teang Pro-oht (or pull the rope - a tug of war)

This is where the big fat western man is the hero. If you're a big fat toad this is your 15 seconds of glory and maybe the key to a young ladies heart. **DO** join in. Perhaps you can extract some payment of beer to join one side. It's simple to play. Two teams with a scarf tied in the middle of the rope pull in opposite directions. **DON'T** expect to do it just once and don't try too hard. Winning isn't the point, having a happy time is.

Khmer dancing

Cambodia has too many traditional dances to describe here. Just remember that they are slow and graceful and very formal. So use the hands and move slowly to the music following your friends who will be so happy that you joined in. Often you move in circles around a table with an arrangement of flowers.

Boys dance with boys and girls with girls or in pairs. You will have to get used to holding hands with same sex partners. When the dance starts the boys will quickly ask the foreign men to dance by bowing and giving a *sompheas*. **DO** get up and follow the boys' lead to the floor and keep smiling and laugh and enjoy. **DON'T** be a wallflower. **DON'T** expect to dance with the opposite sex. There will be a time when the traditional dancing stops and a western rock and roll or a disco number is put on. Now everyone just dances in pairs or alone or whatever and wherever they want.

Sports: volleyball, soccer and badminton

The men in particular love to play these sports especially in the cool of the late afternoon. It is an ideal thing to do, so do join in. Women will often play badminton, which is also great fun.

Singing and karaoke

DO make the effort to be brave and get up to the microphone to sing. Your companions will love it and you will be much appreciated for the rest of your stay. **DON'T** try to tell a joke as the language barrier will kill it. BUT if you can do a comic routine you will be a winner. The Khmer love the old Charlie Chaplin movies and Mr. Bean.

DO join in the fun and if you are a man, give a man who sings well a bunch of flowers (hastily grabbed from anywhere). Hilarious joviality is had by all.

Royal ploughing ceremony - pageantry and astrological predictions

The main ceremony occurs in front of the national museum next to the Royal Palace. Royal oxen are lead in a royal procession around a circular path three times and then let loose on seven golden dishes containing wine, water, rice, maize, sesame seeds, broad beans and grass. The success of the rice crop is based upon what the oxen eat first. If the grains are favoured they will be bountiful the following year. Choosing water means that rainfall will be plentiful. If wine or broad beans are selected doom and gloom are predicted. Khmer pay great attention to the predictions. The ceremony is especially colourful and has an ancient Vedic epic appearance and feel with wonderful golden costumes.

Pchum Ben or festival of the ancestors

In the Buddhist calendar, the first day of the waning moon in October is the beginning of this 15 day ceremony. Worshippers make offerings to their ancestors. For 14 days Buddhists take food to the monks.

Khmer ancestors chose this month as it is the most difficult time for monks to find food due to the rainy season which confines monks to their *wats*. On the 15th day, Buddhists gather at temples to pay homage to departed relatives. Traditional cakes (*nom ansam* and *nom kum*) made from glutinous rice cooked in banana leaves are eaten.

Kathen Tean

During the rainy season monks are restricted to the *wats* for three months. After this time Buddhists raise funds to buy the monks basic necessities to rebuild, or renovate, the pagodas that were destroyed by the KR. Families put on ceremonial banquets at their homes and invitees pay a donation. A poor *wat* is selected, often in a distant province. The patrons of the *Kathen* earn great *Karma*. All *wats* have donation boxes and can receive *Kathen* donations once annually. If you are invited to a *Kathen* do go and note that while it is not an official holiday, offices will close during this time.

Bon Oum Tuk - the water festival - the annual colour and pageantry to celebrate the changing direction of the Tonle Sap River

The festival also commemorates the defeat of the Chams by the Khmers in the 12th century. Held over 3 days, the festival celebrates the reversal of the Tonle Sap River as its waters flow from the lake into the Mekong

River. The festival is held to celebrate and pray for the happiness of the people and for abundant rain to grow rice next year.

Boat races are held on the river in front of the Royal Palace for 3 days. The fastest boats (called *pirogue*) from the provinces located along the rivers and lake, come to Phnom Penh for the contest. Various ministries also compete. Both men and women race but not against each other. There are two types of boat; the *oum* which are free-paddled, and the *cheiw* which use a paddle and a rollick. These boats are housed in the *wats* and can be seen at temples like Wat Botum Vathey. They are made from special wood called *korki* which is specially grown in the grounds of *wats*.

The event always coincides with the full moon of the windy month in the lunar calendar and is the best time of year to visit Cambodia and Phnom Penh as the rains have just ended and the weather is cooler and fresh. Fields are a rich green and everyone is happy and preparing for the harvest season. Soon the fishing season will open and a time of plenty is around the corner. Huge crowds converge on Phnom Penh so whole sections of the city near the Royal Place and river are closed to traffic. The municipal government spends a large amount to clean the city and erect lights and displays and pays for the colourful floats on the river at night and the fireworks.

There are numerous parties, open-air concerts and HUGE CROWDS. TAKE NOTE - HUGE CROWDS IN PHNOM PENH. The crowds are peaceful but the sheer numbers mean that you can get crushed and separated from your friends. **DO** take special care with children who are very vulnerable. If you hate crowds then it may be best to leave Phnom Penh for the provinces or beach or visit a neighbouring country as many foreign residents do.

The police will make efforts to ensure safety. Ambulances are stationed on the streets. There is a great party atmosphere as the boat crews compete for regional pride and prizes. However, the point is not to find one winner. Everyone who competes is considered a winner even though formal winners in each category are announced.

In this ceremony, magnificently colourful boat races are held on the river in front of the Royal Palace, attended by the King and numerous dignitaries. There are hundreds of boats that must first row upstream to the Japanese bridge. This is very exhausting indeed so beware if you are asked to help crew a boat. For the return they race with the current in pairs at full speed to the finish line in front of the royal pavilion. The highlight comes on the last evening when all boats in full regalia row upstream and then turn and float downstream past the King with oarsmen standing upright, oars held vertically, in a massive display of brilliant colour. Immediately after this the sun sets in the west over the Royal Palace and the full moon rises in the east across the river from Phnom Penh. Fireworks go off and colourful floats begin slow circles up and down the river until about 10 p.m. It is a great and beautiful celebration.

Where to view the Boat Festival

Since the festival is on the river in front of the Royal Palace you should try any one of the restaurants facing the river. The Foreign Correspondents Club of Cambodia (FCCC) has one of the best locations for photography from its top deck. If you go to the restaurants catering for foreigners you are likely to have a pleasurable time in the party atmosphere. If you want action photographs of the boats at river level then you will have some fun getting through the crowds along the promenade on the river bank. The local TV stations carry impressive coverage as they have cameras on helicopters and boats on the river.

CEREMONIES-
WEDDINGS, FUNERAL

Cambodia

Weddings

Now that Cambodia is enjoying peace after so many years of suffering, the Khmers are eager for happiness and to restart their lives and families. Given that Cambodia is experiencing a baby boom and there are so many young people, there are lots of couples marrying. For a foreigner this means many very noisy celebrations that start very early in the morning. There will also be road closures and traffic jams as the wedding processions take to the streets, wedding celebration parties and the giving of financial gifts.

DO take lots and lots of photos. Get photos of everyone, especially formal snaps of you with the couple. Photos of you giving the "pink envelope" stuffed with your cash gift, are also fun. If you want to make a show of it **DO** hold the envelope high above your head and make the groom lift the bride to get it. Photographers and video crews are invited. **DO** dress up in your most glamorous clothes and put on all your jewellery. **DO** expect lots of smiles and beautiful people in their party best.

The date and timing of the wedding is very important so relatives will consult with monks to ascertain the most auspicious time. Astrology will be used to determine the date and to ensure the compatibility of the bride and groom. The calendar consists of a 12 year cycle in which each year is associated with an animal and this is the basis of determining compatibility. I am a rabbit and my wife is a monkey, which is fine. So do ask about what animal the bride and groom are as it is always safe to joke about this and say what a good match it is.

Weddings are also associated with very bawdy times: dirty jokes about honeymoons and sex. Now "the couple is marrying taboos" are out. Often weddings involve a special comic act with a man and a woman doing a stand up comic routine with lots of sexual innuendo or direct jokes. Now is the time for living together and starting families. So do laugh even if you can't follow – you will get the drift.

The wedding season

Cambodia has two distinct seasons – the dry season (from November to April) and the rainy season (from May to December). As with everything else in Cambodia, especially major social events, the weather has a big impact. Thus it is usual and preferred for Khmer marriages to be held in the cool dry season after the rains have abated. So weddings are plentiful between November and March. Great numbers of wedding parties can be seen across the country with bride and groom posing for formal photographs in the most pretty places available – parks, flower gardens, along river banks and at temples, etc. Wedding cars and processions are common sights: white cars with big red bows.

The pink envelope - do go if formally invited

Weddings are announced by the delivery of pink perfumed envelopes – "the pink envelope" as foreigners call it. In traditional

Khmer culture they are delivered personally and when delivered the recipient is expected to commit to attending. Relatives cannot just put them in the post (which doesn't exist in most places remember) or call friends on the phone (although phone access is increasing exponentially). Weddings are very important and unlike in the west, **DO** be clear with your friends whether you can or cannot attend. It is really desirable to attend. **DO** expect to have people taking many days off making guest lists and delivering the invitations.

The street procession

The traditional wedding ceremony lasts three days but is now usually compressed into two. Poorer families or those wanting a shorter service may take one day with no party. If the families are rich and powerful the wedding can be huge involving thousands of

guests. The rich and famous will have the biggest parties you will ever see. Ambassadors and royalty may be invited and no expense is spared. Khmer culture places great emphasis on family relationships so the ruling rich and elite are busily consolidating their hold on power and guaranteeing loyalty by marrying their children off to each other. At the highest level this is very significant.

If you are unlucky enough to be next door to a wedding you will have no trouble knowing. The street will be blocked for a night and day or two and there will be lots of music.

On the first day (perhaps in early morning or in the afternoon) monks will be invited. Offerings of fruit and food are made by the groom to the bride's family who are asked if they consent to the marriage. There are some important moments during the wedding

ceremony when you will be invited to participate - **DO** participate. **DO** make a ceremonial cutting of the hair of the bride and groom. **DO** tie a red string around the wrist of the couple and do make a wish for them. Follow your Khmer friend's lead. **DO** wish the couple happiness, long life and good health and of course lots of children – especially if the bride is very young and pretty.

The next day the groom's party lines up along the street outside the bride's home usually in the early morning (peak hour in Phnom Penh but stuff the traffic and hey, it's a big day and if police are involved for bigger parties they will direct or block traffic) and then proceeds to the bride's house. Traditionally both bride and groom are dressed in magnificent costumes out of ancient Vedic epics like the Ramayana. They are king and queen for the day. **DO** make sure you are on time.

The wedding venue

It is a common sight for at least half a street to be blocked off the night before the wedding procession is to take place. These are easily recognised by the entrance, which will have banana trees on either side with bunches of bananas, one silver and one gold, with a picture of a bride and groom above the entrance. These symbolize wealth and prosperity for the new couple.

The final party and expectations of gifts - the foreigner gives money

Most weddings also involve a party which may be held at the bride's home or at a restaurant. Since weddings are one of the biggest expenses a family will ever undertake **DO** give at least $10 towards the cost of the meal. There will be a table near the door with trusted friends collecting money and recording what has been received. Friends of the couple will give presents and you can too if you feel inclined, but cash is much preferred.

Rich and powerful family weddings are different in that they have so much money they don't need yours. If you are invited it is because you are considered special and your $10 or $20 is irrelevant as other important guests have thrown into a special urn the keys of new Mercedes, Lexuses, Landcruisers and the like. Such families may send their newlyweds overseas for the honeymoon.

DO expect the bride to change at least 7 to 10 times into wonderful gorgeous gowns and do expect loud (maybe very very loud) music. More expensive weddings will also hire bands with very beautiful singers.

The cutting of the cake is the climax of the party and will be associated with playing of *"Happy Birthday in English"* as families do not have a western wedding song to play. So if you are in the bathroom and hear Happy Birthday being played, **DO** hurry up and get back to stand and clap and **DO** take photos. There will be bon bon crackers that are set off by pulling a string sending streamers into the air; and spray cans of bright coloured spaghetti.

Wedding parties are formal so you should dress very nicely. Khmer girls and ladies will spend the whole day preparing for the event and weeks beforehand getting clothes made. **DO** dress in your very best. The couple will greet you at the entrance formally along with the bridesmaids and groomsmen. You should offer a formal *sompheas* greeting to the bride and groom and shake hands with the groom. **DON'T** try kissing the bride. Later on the couple will be given a very small morsel of food to bite from at the same time, thus forcing their lips together. **DO** have your camera ready as this is a popular stunt. You will be led to a table for the meal and you should sit where you are directed to. Typically there are 8 or 10 to a table and efforts will be made to place you with other foreigners so you can speak English. You will have to wait until the table is full before the food is served.

Remember, these parties start and finish quite early unlike at home. Arriving at 8pm is too late. So **DO** be on time, usually 5-6 pm.

DON'T expect rituals like throwing the bouquet and don't try and organise stag parties and hen nights. **DON'T** get drunk as this will not be appreciated.

Funeral

Like weddings, funerals are of great importance and should naturally be afforded all due respect and attention. The feeling and its intensity will change according to the situation and nature of the death – whether by natural causes and old age or accident, illness or act of violence. What to do? **DO** know that if invited you must attend and give a financial gift at the funeral gathering as relatives look to their family, friends and neighbours for support.

Your donation is to help with the general costs. You don't have to give as much as at weddings and you can contribute in the local currency. Use clean bills: 3 larger denomination notes of R10,000 or higher are a good idea. Three is a special number (as in Christianity - Father, Son and Holy Ghost).

There are several parts to a funeral. First, the body will lie at the home (in most cases) or at the pagoda (if the deceased died of illness or violence or a road accident or if the family is poor). There will be a procession to the *wat* for cremation or burial in a crypt, followed by a wake at home. It is considered bad luck to have the deceased at home if the death was due to violence or a traffic accident. Funerals are announced by some of the loudest music you may ever hear in Cambodia. **DON'T** be shocked if you are awoken at 4am by very loud wailing and music. A death is being announced through PA systems set up in the street. Special mourners will be engaged and they do wail and weep. This ear drum splitting wailing will continue for some days, 7 in some cases. If you are in an hotel or office nearby your work may just have to stop. Nuns will be engaged as advisors to take care of ceremonial details such as the laying of the corpse and placement of flowers. Monks will come later to bless the deceased, while the actual cremation will be performed by others.

If the family can afford it, the funeral wake will last 7 days. Poorer families will hold a wake for just 3 days and then again on the 7th day. The wake is less important unless you are close to the family. There will be another ceremony 100 days later. Then, at the Pchum Ben festival, friends and relatives will return to the *wats* to pray for their newly deceased and ancestors and to give alms to the monks.

A few tips:

- **DO** afford respect to the funeral procession even if the traffic is completely blocked off and you are going to be very late.

- When you go to your friend's house **DO** remember to take your shoes off and do go inside to see the altar and to express your condolences. The deceased may be lying in a coffin. The family will decide with the advice of the monks

when to seal the coffin. There will be a photo of the deceased with offerings of flowers and incense. **DO** light 3 sticks of incense and **DO** place flowers when at the altar.

- Women are not restricted in any way as to attendance at any parts of the ceremony.

- **DO** accept the red twine offered to you on arrival at the house – it is to ensure you **DON'T** incur bad luck by being in the presence of the dead. You can put it in your pocket or if you wish, tie it around your wrist.

- **DO** bow and greet the nuns with a *sompheas* and do sit where you are shown. You are not expected to stay for very long.

- Unlike western funerals there are no eulogies so **DON'T** get up and give one.

- **DON'T** get drunk it is very much unappreciated.

- Men, **DO** wear a white shirt and black pants. Ladies, **DO** wear a modest white blouse and black dress and obviously not too much makeup.

- If you feel upset **DON'T** hold back your tears as emotions are appreciated.

- If you are offered food then **DO** consume it before you depart as this is polite.

PUBLIC PLACES

Cambodia

Do relax, enjoy and smile

Cambodia is a charming, fascinating place. If you keep smiling and keep your wits about you, a pleasant stay is guaranteed. The Khmer are not known for exerting themselves with trouble and fuss, so why should you? It is a hot country so people make great efforts to avoid heat in the body and mind. So **DON'T** get flustered in the hot sun.

Photography and video recording

DO take lots of photographs. One of the great pastimes in Cambodia is photography. Weddings and parties are times for masses of snaps and videos. If you are trying to get some close up shots of Cambodians, **DO** ask them for permission. **DO** expect everyone to want to be in the photo and don't expect them to understand the western preoccupation with candid shots and close ups. The Khmer prefer carefully staged formal poses against a nice

backdrop with flowers or some branch in the hand like a palm leaf. Also, full body shots are preferred including the feet and head. **DON'T** crop off someone's head if you want to share the photos with your friends later. Also, know that the numbers 3 and 5 are special. So **DON'T** try to snap 3 or 5 people, as this is considered unlucky. The person in the middle may get sick. There are numerous shops for developing film and making prints, all offering good enough service.

Ride don't walk - avoid exercise

One thing to remember is that the Khmer are not known for exercise and getting hot and sweaty. They don't like to go for a walk so almost everyone gets a ride or uses a vehicle. Whole families (of up to seven or more people) can be seen driving on one motorbike. Pigs are also often seen trussed and riding pillion. Young children ride bicycles and everybody else cars or the traditional cyclo (a rickshaw) although these are becoming less common as the relentless drive for faster motorbikes proceeds.

If someone asks you if you want a *"dahleng"* (literally walk play or promenade) **DON'T** get confused. It is not "darling" or an offer of romance or sex.

Early rising

Traditionally the Khmer get up quite early before sunrise and do like to exercise in the cool of the morning or late afternoon. In fact the usual workday in Cambodia starts at 7 or 7:30 am, not 8 or 9 am as in the west. So do get up early.

Internet cafes and email

The internet age has come to Cambodia so do expect to see internet cafes wherever you go. Even quite remote areas are getting wired which makes staying in touch with your friends so easy. In Siem Reap, every second building is an internet joint.

ACCOMMODATION

General considerations

DO follow basic common sense and check things out first when selecting a place to stay. A hotel may have some good rooms and some real disasters. Some travellers will say a hotel is a real brothel whereas someone who stayed in another room was very happy with their stay. **DON'T** assume that everything works – check the toilets, taps, etc. In the major cities most people have no problems most of the time, but you can't be sure.

There are hotels catering for different groups – the top end of the tourist market, those who want a family atmosphere for children, those that cater for backpackers, etc. The rules vary. For example, in higher class places female guests will have to be signed in as in other countries. **DO** respect notices like no "gambling, no prostitution, no drugs, etc." They are there for a reason: to protect you, a valued guest, and the reputation of the hotel.

Watch your expectations of service

Cambodia is making great strides to improve its tourist facilities and the pace of change is very rapid, but do beware. **DO** keep smiling and ask for things you need. **DO** be patient as it might take time for them to arrive. The Khmer staff want to help but may not understand what you are talking about. If you are wanting better service **DON'T** be uncharitable. Cambodia has just opened up for tourists and is learning how to serve you the way you expect. Things like dry cleaning may be best left for later although the bigger hotels can do it.

Safety tip: DO keep your wits about you if you are one to go for a walk after dinner at night alone in the park outside your hotel. The park at Wat Phnom (the heart of Phnom Penh) is NOT safe at night. After all if you were a robber wouldn't you prey on slow moving rich foreigners who don't know the street rules and who are carrying big easily snatched bags with money and cameras?

Some other tips:

- **DO** expect power cuts often at the most inconvenient times like when you are naked with soap on your face in the shower. **DO** carry a small torch and candles plus lighter.

- **DO** watch your head. The Khmers are shorter than many westerners. Rooms are not built to take your height into account. Especially annoying head bumping places are stairwells and bathroom doors. **DO** try to remember this when you get up in the early hours (especially if you sleep with all lights off) to go to the bathroom.

- **DO** expect to have problems with electrical connections and power sockets. There is no standard power socket and plug, so **DO** carry your adapter set. If you need one the hotel can often oblige as everyone has problems connecting. The standard voltage is supposed to be 240V and usually is but it does vary.

- **DO** watch your feet as steps can be tiny. This can lead to bruising situations when you're watching your step and trying not to decapitate yourself on low slung doors and ceilings.

Hotels and guest houses

Cambodia is keen to maximise (exploit to the maximum) the opportunity afforded by being home to one of the "seven wonders of the world" as well as many other temples. In fact the Government is pinning its hopes on a tourist boom. As this book goes to press there is a massive hotel building boom in Siem Reap and Phnom Penh. So do expect lots of new hotels to be available that are not listed in older guide books. As their numbers grow, the

competition between hotels will intensify. **DO** look out for special offers in guidebooks, the local press or just pinned to walls. **DO** ask your fellow travellers.

Hotels range from 5-star (although the service is not as you would get in 5-star hotels in more mature destinations like Bangkok or Singapore) to the cheap $3 guesthouse with few or no amenities. The choice is up to you. **DON'T** waste your money in a top of the line hotel, as the difference in cost between a perfectly adequate 2-3 star hotel is great. Also **DON'T** waste your cash in your home country getting tour operators to book, as the mark up is big. Instead, **DO** use the internet to search for hotels before you arrive and once in country **DO** ask your fellow travellers for tips. Even small, modest places have home pages that allow you to make a reservation by fax or email.

Obviously if you are away from the bigger tourist areas and exploring the country then **DO** expect some adventures with the village accommodation. It is possible to find accommodation in a village house in the countryside but do expect to rough it.

If you are in the countryside and even in the towns **DON'T** forget a mosquito net, torch, candles and toilet paper. Remember the Khmer are shorter than you and the beds mattresses may be short and the mosquito net tight. So do put something

between your body and the net so pesky mosquitoes can't get at you through the net. **DO** expect to have to curl up if you are tall. **DO** expect to bathe in very basic conditions. **DO** be aware of wildlife especially cockroaches, scorpions, centipedes and mosquitoes. **DO** take your flashlight and check the outhouse floor before you squat down. **DON'T** walk barefoot outside.

Geckos are a common sight in Cambodia. There are two main types - the smaller critters (about 10 cm long) that have a soft chirping sound and have the annoying habit of dropping their pellets on your toothbrush, pillow or computer keypad, etc. but are harmless and the much larger beasts (roughly 30 cm. long) that are ugly and hiss and look threatening. The smaller animals (called *jingjoh* in Khmer) scamper about and eat flies and mosquitoes, which is great, so don't hurt them - they are your friends. The larger animals called (*Ta kie* in Khmer) do bite if you try and catch them so if lizards are your thing, **DO** put on a sock or glove before you grab it. The good news is that the larger animals are very shy and often make their existence known by a very loud distinctive call. So **DON'T** freak out when a large gecko lets forth with its call which can be VERY VERY loud if close by or in an enclosed room. These friendly creatures freak out European (and other) visitors who have never had a reptile in their homes before or who have phobias. One popular game is to count "virgin, not virgin,

virgin, etc." at each call with reference to your friend.

I remember one wonderful evening when I was accompanying a young Indian husband and wife. We stayed in a provincial guesthouse in adjacent rooms with adjoining plywood sound-reflecting ceilings. The husband was a very unworldly and clumsy man who snored loudly. It was late and the lights were off (maybe the generator was turned off) and the husband was keeping the entire floor awake with his blissful snoring. Suddenly it happened, a huge beast let forth with GHECKO, GHECKO, GHECKO. It sounded really loud because of the hard plywood

ceilings and closed space. The wife screamed and called her husband to help. The husband was awakened, snorting loudly and struggling to gain consciousness promptly fell out of bed in the darkness and bedlam set in – we laughed for days – but not the wife who was really scared.

Good news for asthmatics. If this is an affliction you suffer from, then **DO** eat 3 large dried geckos – the whole thing – tip of the nose to the claws and tail. If your asthma returns eat a lizard. Traditional medicine shops sell them gutted and stretched out. Due to their medicinal properties village people catch and sell them for $0.12.

DO check out rivers, ponds and water courses before bathing. If the water is clean and flowing and the bottom sandy then you are probably OK. The crazy folk who live in Phnom Penh stage an annual cross Mekong swim upriver of the capital city in December (when the river is at a low point and the current is not so strong)

and injuries and infections are very rare if they occur at all. So if you want an exotic one of a kind souvenir then do join the swim for the memorial T-shirt. **DON'T** bathe if there is a bad odour and cows are around – there are leeches and rare tropical infections. **DON'T** worry about crocs in most rivers as they have all been eaten. There are no piranhas, just rare fish diseases.

Assistance with taxis and airport rides, etc.

DO ask your hotel or guesthouse for a ride to the airport as even smaller guesthouses will be able to arrange whatever you need most of the time. Cambodia has a taxi boom with masses of Toyota Camrys waiting to whisk you to your destination. The usual daily hire rate is US$20 - $25 plus petrol if you are going out of the city. Airport rides should be no more than $5 - $6. Motorbike taxis are also readily available for say $8 per day in Siem Reap.

Where to stay

This is obviously up to you. **DO** check out the tourist guidebooks when you arrive at the airport. These are free and have pretty good maps and information. **DO** confer with fellow travellers. If you want noisy, busy, glitzy places located in central Phnom Penh close to the markets on the busy main streets, then you will not be disappointed. But if you want some more atmosphere then do go for places along the river.

In Siem Reap there are many choices and the choices are increasing daily. Note that the town of Siem Reap is fairly small with not much to do apart from visiting the temples. Most of the four and five star hotels are on the edge of town and devoid of nightlife. **DON'T** stay there if you like to wander around at night, pop into bars and shops and feel that you are not the only person in town. Instead, **DO** stay downtown near the old market in one of the several basic but clean guesthouses.

The coastal areas of Kampong Som, Kampot and Kep, and Koh Kong have two main choices, well three actually - hotels/guest houses on or near the beaches, hotels/guest houses in the town centre (boring but cheaper and closer to the markets if you must shop on a beach holiday) and gambling casinos in Kampong Som and Koh Kong if this is your thing. Casinos have good accommodation.

Tap water - don't drink it

Most foreigners find cleaning their teeth in the tap water presents no problems in the cities most of the time. To be extra sure, rinse your mouth with drinking water after brushing. But **DON'T** ever drink it. Some people are afraid to take the chance even with brushing their teeth. Hotels will often provide one or two bottles of drinking water free per night with the room. If you want to buy a supply, bottled water is readily available at 6 litres for a buck for the cheapest kind in opaque soft plastic bottles. The various brands in clear harder plastic containers are more expensive but that doesn't provide a better guarantee of quality.

Language problems

DO expect to have communication stuff ups. Do keep smiling at all times and persist patiently. On the other hand, **DO** be suitably impressed by the linguistic abilities of tour guides. To be a registered guide the boys and girls must go to a tourism college and learn a second language well. Their proficiency in English, Spanish, Portuguese, French and Mandarin often surpasses what you find elsewhere in Southeast Asia.

Safekeeping

You will have to be the judge. Generally it is safer to keep your valuables in your hotel than to risk losing them from a pickpocket.

It depends on your lifestyle and accommodation. If you are going to be spending time out at night and coming back late, then don't carry lots of cash. Since credit cards are of limited use and there are no ATMs offering access to international accounts, **DO** keep them locked up with your passport in your hotel room inside your suitcase or hotel safety deposit box. If you want to change air tickets or cash travellers cheques or get a cash advance from a credit card then you will need to take your passport.

FOOD AND
RESTAURANTS

Cambodia

Don't eat alone

Food and dining together are very important for the Khmer who love to eat and feast together and who go out in large family groups to restaurants and cheaper roadside markets. Khmers usually have three meals per day but they nibble anytime. Maybe this is why there are many feast days in the Cambodian calendar, where there are a lot of different kinds of food to eat. Some of these occasions are weddings, funerals, parties, a baby's first month, birthdays, Pchum Ben (festival of the ancestors), Khmer New Year (when a visit to a Pagoda is also required) or picnics. The list goes on and on.

DON'T be surprised if you go to a restaurant alone to be looked at in bewilderment. The Khmer cannot understand why anyone would eat alone. **DON'T** think of taking one friend to a nice expensive restaurant for a meal together – very unhappy just 2 people. The Khmer would prefer to go out in a larger group to a cheaper place and enjoy together.

Traditional Cambodian food can be very good as the country

has such ideal natural conditions for agriculture. **DO** expect the basics, rice and fish, with many wonderful fresh spices, ginger, comfrey, mint, lemon grass, basil and many many more. Khmer food is not spicy like Thai food so if you are a lover of hot spices you will have to add some chilli sauce or fresh chillies. If you are a vegetarian do expect to be frustrated at the choices because the

Khmer can't understand why you don't eat meat. Monks eat all meats.

If you want to live on the wild side, ask your friends to do the ordering. If you can eat pretty much anything then this is what you may get: guts soup, fried chicken feet, small shrivelled up little birds that are nice and crunchy (and very expensive), fertilised eggs that may test your ability to not throw up... The list goes on to include endangered species like turtles and snakes. **DO** your bit and say no when offered them and explain that you want to help protect the planet. **DON'T** expect your friends to understand though. There are many tasty local snacks such as fried crickets, fried silkworm pupae, large huntsman spiders on skewers, water beetles, dung beetles and more. Bon appetite!!

Real meal and rich people eat meat

The Khmer feel that a real meal must be heavy with meat. This is especially so if you are in the company of high ranking military gentlemen or policemen. The meal may well include lots of wild game such as deer (with a few endangered animals served up) and lots of whisky and beer. Rice will be served last. They want you to know they are big shots and thus show their status with an expensive meaty meal.

MSG (monosodium glutamate) is a problem as the Khmer, along with many Asian people, think of it as the king of spices. They cannot understand our concern. If you do get headaches from MSG then do try and say *"som kom da bijeng"* (or please don't put MSG). It may be easier to say "no ajinomoto please" or "no seasoning please". Good luck.

Do stop for lunch and breakfast too

If you are travelling with your Khmer friends **DO** understand that you must stop for lunch at 12 noon. **DON'T** try to get around this. Day trips will be planned with the implicit knowledge that you will start early, say 6am, so as to be able to stop soon after you have gotten started (at 7am) at a roadside restaurant for breakfast, and then again at 12 noon for lunch, followed by a siesta (in a hammock is ideal).

Do go on picnics

Cambodians frequently have picnics. Entire families go to beautiful places in the countryside and spend the day eating together, sleeping, drinking, playing cards and sport. Favourite places include the beach, parks, rivers, lakes and the mountains or at

Angkor Wat. Food is prepared by hand or a stove is taken along to cook on. People eat grilled, fried or barbecued meat, rice, bread, lots of fruit, beer, soft drinks and one or two kinds of dessert. The ideal Khmer pastime may appear to westerners to be a big meal in a large group followed by a siesta in a hammock – *sabai sabai*. **DON'T** be surprised to find people resting under trees in hammocks everywhere. You may wonder at times if anyone works.

A picnic at the seaside usually involves a lot of seafood. Crabs, lobsters, prawns, squid and fish are consumed in great quantities along with beer, wine or whisky. Women usually don't drink alcohol, preferring instead soft drinks or coconut juice.

So seafood lovers, this is for you. **DO** head for the beaches, Kampong Som and Kampot (Kep) are especially popular. Kep is much less developed than Kampong Som and has different attractions including lots of delicious crabs.

DO join in the picnic. It is the ideal way to get to see some lovely areas and get to know your hosts. **DON'T** be surprised and/or disappointed if you find the popular picnic places trashed with garbage.

Eating at your friend's house

DON'T forget to take off your shoes before entering and **DON'T** step on the threshold.

Cambodians do not usually have a dining room. Traditionally they eat on the floor on a mat in the living room or under the

house if it is on stilts especially in the hot season. In these modern times some will eat at a table. All the dishes are put on the mat at the same time and everyone helps himself or herself to the food. Traditionally, Cambodian people eat with their right hand, but most now use a spoon and fork. After the meal, dessert is taken, often fruit together with tea or boiled water.

When guests arrive for dinner special food is usually prepared. Cambodian cooking is the responsibility of the women and the oldest woman has the most responsibility. She supervises the younger ladies and decides on the daily meals. When the food is ready to eat, the oldest people (usually the parents) begin first and then everyone joins in. **DO** take the water, tea or food offered to you. **DON'T** wait for your hosts to start - they await your lead as honoured guest. It can be a little awkward if everyone is sitting in silence waiting for you to start.

Remember **DON'T** sit with crossed legs when you are talking to others. **DO** sit on the mat in your appointed place with your feet to your side and **DO** express your satisfaction with the meal

and **DO** complement the cooks (the women). Here is a tip if this is too painful or uncomfortable: try to sit with your back against a wall. This way you can lean back and take the pressure off the knees. Your hosts will be understanding, so if it is hard for you, ask if you can sit on a chair. Your hosts will happily oblige.

You **DON'T** have to help the owner of the house set up the table or clean up and do the dishes after the meal.

DON'T arrive empty handed. Bring seasonal fruits or drinks (alcoholic for the men and worldly ladies and non alcoholic for the other women and children). If you are vegetarian do tell your host ahead of time as they really want you to have a happy meal.

Noodles are eaten with a fork and spoon or chopsticks. **DON'T** make noises like slurping and burping or pinging your utensils on the plates or glasses, as this is considered impolite. Flatulence is also impolite and will probably result in a shriek of laughter from the children present (the Khmer word is *poum*).

Eating in restaurants and hotels

DO follow the lead of those around you if in doubt. Obviously you may not find the food you are used to and may have to be flexible and patient. **DO** expect language problems so ask for a menu. It is common to have menus with photos to help you choose.

Voice tone

DO speak with a smile and never get cross and complain loudly. It may be frustrating at times but chalk it up to experience.

Patience and tolerance

DO be patient and do expect the waitress to try and help but

DON'T expect top service. There is such an explosion in tourism that many businesses are opening, providing employment for young men and women. But they may not really have much clue about what foreigners like and expect.

Who pays?

DO remember that the Khmer really love to go out in large groups and the custom is that the person who does the inviting pays. Take care as it can be upsetting and you may feel used and exploited if it's your suggestion. If you ask a friend out he or she may bring a friend or two and since you are paying they will order expensive food and lots of drinks. Guys, **DON'T** expect to be able to meet some nice girl and ask her to a romantic dinner for just the two of you. If you are already an item then yes she will go with you alone. But in the beginning she will bring at least one girl friend and maybe a brother, a friend and his cousin, all of

whom will order the most expensive menu items. They want to show you off: you are a big rich man. The Khmer do understand the concept of going dutch, if this is agreed ahead of time. So **DO** be clear beforehand. If you are travelling and having lunch by necessity together, then people will pay for their own meals.

Tipping

You don't have to give significant tips as you do in the U.S. So don't think in terms of 5 or 10 percent. Just the loose change (in *riel*) will do or a few dollars if it is a bigger meal.

SHOPPING IN CAMBODIA - BUYER BE AWARE

Shopping can be great fun so do go and have a look. The markets in Phnom Penh and Siem Reap especially, offer rich experiences. For example, the old market in Siem Reap is like Aladdin's cave with colourful exotica and handicrafts piled from floor to ceiling. There are convincing 'new antiques' that will look wonderful back home, as well as practical things like carved chopsticks, and beautiful silks fashioned into inexpensive cushion covers. **DO** support the aid projects that have trained Cambodians in the traditional arts of stone carving, wood work, dyeing, weaving, etc., and that produce

fabulous handicrafts at ridiculous prices as well as reviving the old skills which mean so much to the country as it rediscovers it roots and traditions.

There are many beautiful and genuinely Cambodian items to be found and many of the predictable scams. Keep smiling and take it easy. As you would do anywhere, do some research first if you are interested in more expensive items, especially gems and antiques.

Some genuine Cambodian items include:

• The *Krama* – a unique locally made checkered scarf which is cheap and may be your first purchase.

• Cambodia has a rich tradition of brilliant hand woven silks and textiles. Note that many so called Thai patterns and designs are in fact Khmer. Many people love to buy these silks and have them tailored into clothes as it costs a fraction of what you pay back home.

• Silver coated ornamental items and animals.

• Betel nut boxes that make great jewellery boxes.

• There are many traditional carvings, paintings, sculptures and rattan items.

Currency

DO remember that US dollars are the notes of choice. Thai baht is also equally accepted. If you are clever and/or lucky you may profit from changing dollars to baht in Thailand and then buying in baht in Cambodia

Prices and bargaining

DO bargain and do expect some exceptional buys. Cambodia is now manufacturing clothes for big international chains and extra stock is sold off in the local markets. If you are careful and well informed you can get real cotton shirts of famous brand names for a few dollars.

Generally no problems

One saving grace about shopping is that most of the time there are no great problems as the sellers are keen to get the cash flow. So don't panic if the seller doesn't have change and quickly disappears out the back of the shop with your big note. S/he is going to another stall to change it.

Jewellery and precious gems - sapphires and rubies

Cambodia is rightly famous for its rubies and sapphires but do be especially careful. High quality rubies are very expensive and the seller knows the price. Most of the best stones from the famous gem city of Pailin are taken to Thailand. Gold is the same price as anywhere else but labour is much cheaper. **DO** consider getting new settings for your gems but get reliable references for the shop before leaving some precious possession in the care of the goldsmith. **DON'T** expect to be able to get gems certified in government regulated shops, as this service has yet to be developed.

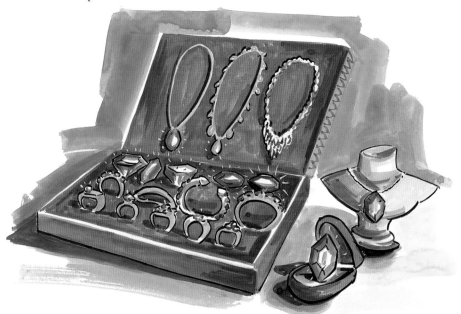

Copyright law and law on intellectual property

Cambodia is now enforcing copyright and intellectual copyright laws. **DO** support this by not shopping for illegal CD's, movies, and software as this will help ensure the growth of industry and jobs, which are critical for the nation's development.

Shipping goods home

This can be done but is very hazardous and best avoided. Do take your purchases with you.

TRAVEL

Cambodia

Travelling in Cambodia is a real adventure and can be great fun. There is now great freedom of movement and opportunity for looking around. Get yourself a *krama* and head off. **DO** expect dreadful roads in some cases and backbreaking rides. **DO** remember that river trips afford some of the best travel experiences so consider the boat between Phnom Penh and Siem Reap, the ocean trips to and from Thailand and river trips up and down the Mekong. Freshwater river dolphins can be seen at Kratie north of Phnom Penh. Ethnic minority groups are in the

mountainous
northeast. There are
limited internal flights to some locations such as Siem Reap, Battambang, and Rattanakiri in the far northeast. **DO** know that the maintenance standards of some of the internal carriers are a concern and flights may be cancelled or rescheduled with little

notice. Also know that the safety standards of some boats are a worry as they can be overcrowded and lack safety equipment.

DON'T travel by train as there are real concerns about the lines and equipment. The rail network is also limited.

Border crossings

The two legal crossing points for foreigners on the Cambodian/Thailand border are at Koh Kong and Poipet. The border crossing at Moc Bai on the Vietnam border is also open to foreigners providing they have obtained the appropriate entry/exit documentation in advance.

Travellers are advised not to use the border crossing at Dong Krolor/Veun Kham on the Laos border as it is not a legal international entry/exit point. Additionally, it is in an isolated location 50 km. to the north of the major town of Stung Treng and is not served by public transport of any kind.

As this book goes to press the Government is negotiating with its neighbours to open more border crossings. **DO** check these out before you try some more adventurous overland crossings. **DON'T** try and cross illegally as you may be in deep trouble.

Plan ahead

DO check first, plan your trip and know where you are going. You really must take charge yourself and don't rely on meeting someone who can understand you and read your map.

Drinks

DO carry drinking water with you always, as it is easy to get dehydrated. Drinking water in sealed plastic bottles is readily obtained at many roadside stalls. Generally it is safe to drink if the seal is unbroken. Coconuts make a great drink and are sterile. **DON'T** indulge with the local ice treats.

Touring and trekking - landmines and UXO

Trekkers do beware. Cambodia remains one of the most heavily mined countries in the world and there are more dangers than you may be used to and ready to cope with. **DO** take very serious notice of landmines and

UXO (unexploded ordinance) in the west and northwest of the country along the Thai border. There are no landmines near Phnom Penh and in the eastern areas near Vietnam as the Vietnamese came in quickly and pushed the KR out to the western border areas in a few days. Bombs dating back to the secret US war in the east are still occasionally found but present no problem as they are usually buried very deep.

Hiring motorbikes

Due to the dreadful state of some roads many people prefer to ride motorbikes especially for cross country travel. There are many magical experiences and places to go. Bikes can be readily hired with your passport being left as deposit. In Phnom Penh it is safe to do so. **DO** wear a helmet. **DO** expect to see insects and stones bouncing off your visor. **DO** consider hiring smaller, more comfortable, cheaper and more economical bikes than the big trail bikes, especially if your legs don't reach the ground. There are some really fantastic organised wild bike tours but do know your limits. Easy Rider and Captain America are alive and well in this land of freedom.

Bicycle touring

More and more tourists are exploring Cambodia by bicycle and report great times. So if you like to take the road less travelled more slowly, then do consider this option. I have a lady friend who regularly goes on very long trips with friends and loves it. She takes local taxis part of the way to break the journey up and has no real problems – although getting flat tires in the middle of nowhere has left her stranded for half a day or more. **DO** plan ahead, know where you are headed and know your limits. **DON'T** take chances by riding late at night in remote areas.

Security risks and bandits in some areas

DO take care. Some areas have former soldiers whose main skills were honed in war time. These guys get drunk, lose money gambling and may be tempted to pick on some easy targets to make a living. Great efforts are being made by the Government to make Cambodia safer but not all police and military are assisting as they should. If you are making a long distance trip across the country to the northeast, northwest and north be wise and **DON'T** take unnecessary risks.

Local travel - motor taxis, cyclos and taxis

The main transport options for tourists are the motorbike taxis called motordups, cyclos (French for cycle) and taxis. It is also very easy to hire small vans and buses. **DO** negotiate the fee ahead of time and know where you are going. If you hire a van or bus for a longer trip do make sure that the price covers the fuel and do expect to be asked to pay for the drivers lunch. Best to get this clear from the start although the rules may change. **DO** stick to the agreed fee, which is probably too high anyway.

What street name or number - there are many.

Street names and numbers in Phnom Penh have changed so many times that different generations of maps will have different names. **DON'T** rely on the local driver to know the name or number you have read about in some guide. **DO** be patient and do keep smiling. Remember your breathing as frustration sets in.

HEALTH TIPS

Cambodia

Malaria and dengue fever

DO know the health risks of malaria and dengue fever. The advice from medical doctors experienced in the local conditions is that the visitor who is not going to travel to remote forest areas does not need to take anti malarial prophylaxis.

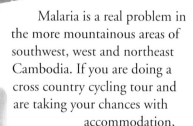

Malaria is a real problem in the more mountainous areas of southwest, west and northeast Cambodia. If you are doing a cross country cycling tour and are taking your chances with accommodation, take a mosquito net and repellent especially in the wet season and more especially just after the rains have abated as the number of mosquitoes increases dramatically with the increase in breeding places. Malaria carrying mosquitoes bite at dusk and at night. **DO** wear socks to thwart the ankle biting pests. Mosquitoes like dark places so white or light coloured socks are better than black. **DO** follow the French fashion of white socks.

If you feel sick and worry that you may have caught malaria **DO** get a check up right away with a competent western trained doctor. The blood test involves a finger prick and is fast. Treatment is also available but take care to get the right stuff. There was a real problem with fake antimalarials a while ago. Early treatment is the way to go.

Dengue (or joint breaking fever) is another story. It is also a mosquito born disease but the "tiger mosquito" or *"moo kham"* as they are known bite in the daytime. It is a larger beast and its striped abdomen is easily seen. It breeds in water so do beware of guesthouses with lots of potted plants. Check if they use *"abate"* which is a chemical put in the water to kill the larvae.

Unfortunately, whereas malaria is not a problem in Phnom Penh and the cities, dengue is.

More health tips

- **DO** be more careful – it is not like home. This is the basic point.

- **DON'T** dally if you get seriously sick or are seriously injured: get yourself to Thailand or Singapore. Medical facilities in Cambodia are getting better, but they have a long way to go. Thailand is the number one medical destination in the region for very good reason.

- **DO** consider buying health and travel insurance. The cost of medical evacuation to Bangkok can be as high as US$15,000 excluding medical treatment.

- **DO** watch the ice in the drinks. There are two kinds of ice easily recognised by their shape: large blocks crushed into smaller

irregular pieces; and rounded ice blocks made in moulds. **DO** take care and consider where you are. If you are in a restaurant in Phnom Penh or a larger tourist centre then the rounded ice blocks are probably OK. But **DON'T** take the risk of the crushed block ice in your drink especially if you are in a village and you can see the blocks being stored in old rice husks on the ground with pigs rooting around in them. If you get sick, **DON'T** just try and soldier on, take care of yourself.

- **DO** be wary of street food especially noodles as the vendor may wash them after boiling in unsanitary water. One of the charming sounds you will hear at night is the rhythmic tapping of the noodle sellers hawking their wares. These vendors carry a small bucket of water to wash the plates and keep using it for the whole time they are out. Take care, the music is lovely but that night maybe spent on the toilet.

- **DO** be careful with minor cuts and abrasions. The tropics are ideal for bugs. Even small wounds can get out of control if you are careless. Many people who spend extended times in the countryside get into problems with small cuts becoming ulcerated or badly infected. This often happens because travellers don't have disinfectant or antiseptic ointment and bandaids. So **DO** travel with a small supply.

SURVIVING A NIGHT
ON THE TOWN

Cambodia

Here are some general tips for both men and women interested in a night out in Cambodia.

DON'T go expecting Phnom Penh nightlife to be like that in Bangkok – it isn't. Yet it is a great town for a night out, from the innocent to the depraved if you wish it.

DO expect an early night if you are in the provinces. Even major tourist areas like Siem Reap and Kampong Som close quite early so you may be hard pressed to find much happening after 10pm. In rural areas, where the majority of the population live, people are up before dawn and asleep quite early.

DO check out traditional music and dance concerts while you are in this wonderful exotic land. The costumes are brilliantly coloured and dancers enchanting.

DO plan your night out especially your travel arrangements - how you'll get there, and how you'll get back (possibly the worse for wear). **DO** remember that as transport options are more limited, you may have to take motordops which is tricky if you have had sixteen whiskies. **DON'T** get on a motorbike if you are drunk and sleepy.

If you are going to be more adventurous and don't have friends to show you around, then **DO** consider arranging a taxi through your hotel. This way you will be sure to get home and if you do have problems with the driver he can be more easily traced. You'll look more like a local resident who knows what he's doing and less like a tourist wandering aimlessly and ripe for plucking!

DO begin the evening by watching the sunset. Phnom Penh's location at the junction of two rivers provides a natural and wonderful place to start the evening. There are many restaurants and cafes offering a fair range of cuisine. Provincial towns often will be located on riverbanks or have parks where people gather in the late afternoon.

DO be friendly with the people you meet. You are likely to be approached by small groups of giggling girls who may be very pretty saying "hello" and "where you come from?" and "what is your name?" Young men will also try to start a conversation. They are just playing and joking and will be offended and upset if you are crude and too forward. Men, don't assume the girls are available, they are just being friendly. If a woman is really available she will make it very clear.

DO expect to be complemented on your long bony nose and white skin. Funny how we all think the other culture is more attractive than our own.

DON'T drink yourself into oblivion: you could be robbed or tricked into parting with your wallet, mobile phone, etc. And if you drink don't drive.

DO look confident and purposeful when you're on the streets rather than a helpless tourist.

DO take with you the name card of where you're staying. The taxi driver may then know exactly where he's supposed to be going.

Money

DON'T take your credit card when you are going out on the town – they are of no use except in the big hotels. So keep them in your hotel and use cash. At least there will be a limit to your spending!

DO hold on to your wallet, mobile phone, camera and so on.

DON'T leave your bag or haversack unattended. In bars, keep hold of it or wrap it round a chair-leg.

DON'T go to the toilet and leave your bag behind.

Pubs and clubs

Cambodia is now developing the pubs and clubs that you find in other major tourist destinations in Asia. There are many bars especially in Phnom Penh along the river front that cater for foreigners. There are of course bars in 5-star hotels and down back streets. They are good places to meet people and not all are girly bars. Foreign women do have a choice if they know the options. The bigger hotels will often have entertainment such as Filipino bands. Many of these bars serve meals.

Beer drinkers take note: **DO** expect beer girls and waitresses to put ice in your beer. Getting an ice cold one without ice is hard. You will have to look for a place with a drink cooler or a fridge. Ice in your drinks is dangerous, especially outside of the major cities.

DO read the daily newspapers, and the freebies available in bars, bookshops, cafes etc. for information on:
- Where to eat and drink;
- What's on;
- Where to listen to live music
- Where to get tickets.....etc.

Nightclubs and girlie bars

Cambodia does have bars and discos but does not have the topless and nude dancing bars of Thailand. There are also "dancing restaurants" (true name) catering mainly for locals. These are places where you sit at a table and drink or eat with your friends and then get up to the dance floor. Hostesses and sometimes gigolos are available at all these places if you want them. Do be careful when buying them drinks as they may order the more expensive cocktails.

Karaoke

Karaoke is great fun and very popular with the Khmer. There are karaoke shops in Phnom Penh and in the provinces ranging from quite sophisticated recording studios to mum and pop restaurants with snacks and drinks. You select a track to sing to by

using the computerised console. Many people love to make a tape to keep. **DO** know that karaoke is not a synonym for sex.

Red lights

DON'T expect distinct red light areas catering for tourists outside of Phnom Penh. Within the city there are a few notorious brothel areas along the northern dyke area (Tuol Kouk) which is now a major city bypass road; and the infamous Svay Pak (or kilometre 11 as it is located 11 km. north of Phnom Penh on Highway 5). These places are seedy and tragic and are now the focus of intense attention by the municipal authorities and may well be closed in the future.

MAINLY FOR MEN

Cambodia

DON'T forget "NUMBER ONE" the condom - the number one rule.

Sex

Let's start at the top of the list and get on with what really matters. Here is a quick quiz for you. What do the following acronyms and terms stand for and really mean: SW, CSW, DSW, IDSW, IFSW, "orange seller girls", *"tuck kalok sellers"*, PGs, Beer Girls, Karaoke girls, MSWM, PLWA, PCFPLWA, HIV/AIDS, RH, ARH, and legally major?

Since sex is such a big topic (anywhere) there are many words for it. SW is "sex worker" (i.e. a person who receives money for sexual services). Being a sex worker means that there is money involved but for some reason some NGOs and health people feel the need to clarify that a SW may not be a CSW "commercial sex worker". You work it out... Next we have a DSW a "direct sex worker" (versus an IDSW an "indirect sex worker"!)

OK so where can you find sex?
SW, CSW and DSW can be found in brothels and massage parlours (sometimes pretending to be barber shops). The implication is that the girl will sleep with any customer. These are limited to Phnom Penh and the major provincial towns.
DON'T expect to find a Patpong, Pattaya, etc. in Cambodia.

Then we have IDSW and IFSW - "indirect sex workers" sometimes known as "informal sex workers" (although they may be very formally dressed in lovely gowns). These terms imply that a SW is not in your face as it were, but someone who may sometimes have sex with a selected customer under some circumstances. IDSW and/or IFSW refer to waitresses and PGS "promotional girls" or "beer girls" who are hired by companies to promote their beer, spirits and wines at restaurants and nightclubs, etc. If the girl likes you she may be available to go with you when she finishes work.

"Orange seller girls" sell oranges in the parks where they will carry baskets of oranges or other fruit. Some may also sell sex if you buy a lot of fruit: all she has in the basket. *Tuck kalok* is a fruit shake. You can specify mixed fruit or just one kind as you wish. You will see many of these fruit shake stalls set up at night in most cities and towns of Cambodia especially near the markets or recreation areas. Some of these stalls are staffed by several pretty girls, who in some cases may be available.

DO remember that Cambodian girls love to dress up and look modern. **DON'T** assume that they are SWs.

If you're gay **DON'T** be shy. Like their Thai counterparts the Khmer are accepting people. The politically correct term in the

NGO and reproductive health world is MSWM "men having sex with men".

DO understand that the Government of Cambodia is concerned not to go the same route as Thailand with its well deserved reputation as the number one destination for sex in Southeast Asia. Recently the Prime Minister issued a sub-decree that all nightclubs and karaoke clubs in the entire country be closed. At the time of writing, karaoke bars were reopening. Some karaoke bars do have hostesses with the mostess, **but** don't get confused – karaoke is not a synonym for sex.

There are also big discussions about Khmer culture being corrupted by Thai movies. **DO** be sensitive to this and understand that Cambodia is not Thailand. You must be well behaved in public places.

One reason for all these concerns is of course HIV/AIDS.

Cambodia does have a serious problem with the highest infection rate in Southeast Asia. Thus we have PLWA "people living with AIDS", and PCFPLWA "people caring for people living with AIDS". Good progress has been made in reducing infection rates but it is very sad and tragic.

So here is the NUMBER ONE DO – **DON'T** FORGET NUMBER ONE. NUMBER ONE is the brand name of a major condom being very actively promoted by people working in RH "reproductive health" and especially ARH "adolescent reproductive health".

Always remember the condom whether with a SW, CSW, IDSW, IFSW or if you are MSWM.

Remember the legal age for prostitution is 18. **DON'T** have sex with children.

What about finding a sweetheart and marriage? **DO** expect to see many lovely girls and exotic damsels who are not SWs and who are open to serious relationships and marriage. **DO** behave as a gentleman should and if your intentions are sincere you may be rewarded with a loving princess.

If you are getting close to a family **DON'T** be surprised if you are asked to adopt someone. It happens and is likely to be a sincere offer. If you are an older person the younger person may be looking for an adopted father. This is a result of the KR period when many people lost their families. It is not an attempt to sell a daughter off and marry her. She may just want the emotional security of having a father.

MAINLY FOR WOMEN

Cambodia

Foreign women are left alone in Cambodia, although there have been cases of assault in both the capital city and in country areas.

The main point for foreign women travelling in Cambodia is to know that it is a male dominated society with great inequities and injustices for women. There is a tragic Khmer saying "men are like gold, women are like cloth", meaning that even if a man has been soiled or muddied (lost his virginity) he can be cleaned but a women once defiled is soiled. **DON'T** expect to be able to change this attitude that will take many years to overcome.

DON'T be surprised if you find a dearth of entertainment and nightlife. If you have come from some of the bigger neighbouring countries you may find yourself frustrated at the choices. Although maybe not – it is very much up to you to make the effort to be adventurous and more flexible.

So what does this mean? If you want to go out at night in Phnom Penh or a major city the choices are limited to bars and restaurants and of course the larger hotels. **DON'T** be surprised if you end up in a man's bar with your male travelling friends watching sport on the tube while the boys down some beer with their Khmer girl friends (or bar girls). You may have to bite your lip as you see some male friend who you know to have a partner or wife and family, playing with a sexy younger girl. If you go out with female friends you may not feel very welcome in some bars. Some western women find it frustrating that the western men seem more preoccupied with the local girls.

Generally it is best to not tempt fate by dressing in sexy outfits – you will attract attention quickly from many Cambodian men who may be hard to get rid of. Most foreign ladies wear simple casual clothes to suit the climate but if you want to wear your favourite little black dress, go for it.

DON'T be surprised if you find it hard to find non-whitening skin care products. Sadly Cambodian women are desperate to lighten their skin. You may have to look hard to get makeup in the colours you are used to. Good hair salons and beauticians are fairly easily found in Phnom Penh but **DON'T** expect to find them in the provinces. Many carry French products. **DO** carry a supply of your favourite shampoo and beauty needs when travelling up country.

DO note however that there are non-girly places catering for the expatriate crowd wanting something other than sex, so make an effort to find them. Get yourself to the riverfront in Phnom Penh and check out calendars for special events and so on. It is fine for a woman to drink alcohol and to drink alone if she wishes. You may also want to visit street 178 which runs next to the National Museum and has many art shops and small galleries. Street 240 which is on the south side of the Royal Palace up to the National Assembly should also be visited as there is a little corner

with nice bookstores, restaurants and bars catering to the expatriate crowd. There are also more opportunities in the bigger tourist areas of Siem Reap and Sihanoukville (Kampong Som). Cambodia is changing fast and trying to make itself more attractive for tourists and residents.

Many women have a great time in Cambodia and come back again and again and make many Khmer friends. If you are into shoes and designing your own clothes there are great possibilities. You can get custom made shoes in Phnom Penh much more cheaply than you can at home. Many women love to buy the brilliant local silks and have clothes made. There are many good tailors both in the capital and provincial towns.

As for men **DON'T** forget "NUMBER ONE" the condom - the number one rule. Always remember safe sex in dangerous times. This may seem obvious and unnecessary to say but remember that any male companion you may meet is most likely to have had sex with others. Remember too that Cambodian men are attracted to western women and that they are likely to have had other lovers.

Exercise a higher degree of personal security awareness

This is obvious advice so no need to make a big deal of it. DO TAKE MUCH MORE CARE THAN YOU WOULD AT HOME - DON'T TEMPT FATE. Here are a few self-evident points.

• **DO** dress modestly, especially in a pagoda.

- **DO** watch out for the charming man with a nice motorbike who wants to take you around - he may be hard to get rid of.

- **DON'T** wear valuables that can be easily grabbed. Snatch and grab thieves on motorbikes in the cities are a threat not just for women but also men.

- **DON'T** show yourself as an obvious and easy target for pickpockets at markets.

- **DO** watch the hot exhaust pipe on right hand side of motorbikes. Many women have a baptism of a serious burn when they first ride motorbike taxis.

- **DO** sit side saddle on motors. This will be one of the new skills you can develop in your travels. Generally women passengers are expected to ride side saddle facing the left of the motor. But if you don't feel safe it is OK to sit straddling the seat as normal. People will understand.

OFF THE RAILS IN
PHNOM PENH

Cambodia

DO know that when travelling you are subject to local laws. A violation of these laws may result in a gaol sentence, served in a local prison, which is a very nasty experience.

The large number of crazy foreigners in Phnom Penh was very striking in the early 1990's but is becoming less so in recent times. Many people were struck by the number of foreigners who had lost the plot. You would see people walking around with the lights on but no one home. Film crews have come and made documentaries about this world, and a book has even been written with the above title *Off the rails in Phnom Penh.* It is wild reading. One proffered explanation for this "phenomenon" is that it results from Cambodia's wild lawless state where you can get away with much more than you can at home, coupled with the beauty and sensuality of the country and people. Another explanation proffered is that the Cambodian people are very accepting and tolerant in many ways and avoid conflict and confrontation allowing cowboys and worse to get away with more than they would be able to at home.

These wild, crazy reckless days are becoming less so. **DON'T** expect to find what you may have heard of before. **DO** know that the Cambodian government is desperately trying to overcome the image of being a dangerous and unsafe place with drugs, underage girls, landmines, KR and criminals. It is projecting itself as a destination for up market tourists who spend lots.

DO watch yourself especially with your own people. Some crazy foreign residents are really brilliant and very interesting in their own right. It is natural to get drawn in by them and to want to help if they are suffering. **DO** be cautious as your own common sense and natural inclinations are not good enough to deal with some cases. Special training is needed to really help some of the disturbed people living in the country. It is not talked about much but there is also a lot of mental illness hidden behind the smiles of the local people too. This is another tragic legacy of the past. **DO** be sympathetic and do be wise and aware of your own limits and abilities to help. There are NGO's offering assistance for the mentally disturbed and you may want to refer your friend there.

DO remember that wild times can be dangerous and that the safety nets in your countries are unknown in Cambodia. Foreigners die in traffic accidents and from drug overdoses. One lucky English lad was saved by a great friend. The unfortunate person took some chemicals and became a crazed lunatic in his guesthouse room and spent the night cutting his credit cards and passports into tiny tiny pieces before lapsing into unconsciousness. A friend got him to Phnom Penh and arranged a replacement passport and a flight home. Others are not so lucky.

DO watch out for the criminal element. If you get involved in smuggling remember there is no honour among thieves. There are some very dangerous criminal gangs operating here with connections in high places, so **DO** beware.

DON'T prey on children for sex. People who do are being caught and imprisoned for very lengthy periods in jails that you would not want to drive by in a bus.

So take note – **DON'T** lose the plot.

Marijuana and yaba (amphetamines)

DO stay away from drugs. Although they are accessible, possession of even small amounts is illegal and are not good for your health!

DO remember the old saying "yous pays your money and yous takes yours chances". Along with Thailand and neighbouring Myanmar there is a growing wave of amphetamine availability which is of great concern to the government and there are growing efforts by many international drug enforcement agencies to fight this. Also take note that there are more and more crackdowns by police which will require bribes for release. Many people were attracted to Cambodia as marijuana was openly sold in large quantities in the local markets, and some restaurants would put some "happy" in their pizza. Sorry to disappoint but this isn't the case now.

BONG does not mean marijuana! A foreign lady who loved to smoke dope recalled that it was "really wild when she first came - like everyone was saying BONG, I mean BONG, everyone was offering me a BONG". "Bong" dear friends, is the Khmer word for older dear friend or older brother/sister. Sorry to disappoint you. Marijuana grows wild and is used by farmers to sedate their poor pigs before they are trussed up and put on motor bikes en route to market. **DO** note that the Hash House Harriers are a social running club for "drinkers with a running problem". Hash is the old English word for army mess hall and doesn't mean dope. So go on the hash for a great run in the countryside around Phnom Penh but **DON'T** expect to smoke intoxicating herbs.

SAFETY TIPS

Cambodia

Here are a few miscellaneous obvious (or should be obvious) safety tips.

- **DO** make sure your passport has at least 6 months left as immigration authorities may deny you entry.

- **DO** stay alert - don't be foolish and don't throw caution to the wind too often or too recklessly. The safety nets of reliable hospitals and trained medical personnel that you are used to at home are not here - especially outside of Phnom Penh.

- **DON'T** ignore the little voice inside. Go with your intuition.

- **DON'T** take pictures of logging trucks, police accepting bribes or beating up demonstrators, or people clearing landmines.

- **DO** pay heed of landmine warning signs - duh.

- **DO** ask the restaurant to organise a reliable motor taxi if in doubt about your security or personal safety when you are leaving late at night. It may cost more but it is safer.

- **DO** consider hiring a taxi in Phnom Penh and get the car to wait. Your hotel can arrange this. It is much better for you to get the English (or French speaking) staff to speak with the driver beforehand and arrange the agreed fee.

- **DO** know where you are going and do get a map. **DON'T** expect the driver to be able to read it.

- **DO** avoid armed drunken soldiers or police. Remember that Khmer men hate to lose face over a woman and expect to control her. If you challenge this power in front of a man's friends his honour is at stake.

- **DON'T** tap a man on the head (even in jest) as this has led to axe murders and grenades being tossed.

A Chinese cook who had been working alongside a Khmer cook for ages and between whom there were lots of jokes and teasing was killed recently when he put a cake on the Khmer cook's head. It was too much. The Khmer cook killed his work mate with a meat cleaver in a rage after stewing over the insult for a few hours. Generally men should not touch women at all.

- **DO** avoid political demonstrations or at least recognise that they are potential flash points between the police/ military and the demonstrators.

- **DO** be very careful with mob violence and street justice. If you are the target of a mob **DON'T** expect the police to intervene and **DON'T** get caught up with thoughts like "the rule of law".

- Traffic accidents. **DO** expect a large crowd to gather fast if there is a road accident. If you are involved keep smiling and **DON'T** get angry. **DO** expect to have to negotiate compensation.

DO expect the police to try to broker this and inflate it to get commission. **DO** expect to have to sit there for a long time. If you keep smiling and stick to your guns and don't yield to outrageous extortion it will be OK.

• **DO** be savvy, **DO** be aware, but **DON'T** let anxiety or paranoia spoil what will certainly be a peaceful holiday in Cambodia. It is unfortunate to have to write this but guns are still too prevalent as a result of the wars and lawless past. Shoot outs do happen and you must take care. If you are unaccustomed to guns and the like you may not have the right reflexes. If you see people running away in fear and/or hitting the deck **DO** TAKE COVER. **DON'T** stick your head up if there is shooting. **DO** take special care to avoid sitting near armed soldiers and/or police at nightclubs who are drinking.

• True story: I was having dinner with my wife and two of our young children in a restaurant on the road along the river front in Phnom Penh at about 7:30pm. This is peak time for dining and a very popular area for Khmers and foreigners. The restaurant was on a street corner and we were at a table on the footpath at most 4 meters from the curb. Suddenly a young woman came running into the restaurant crying "help me" in Khmer. I heard what sounded like firecrackers. I saw another woman crouching down at the curb protecting a child and I thought someone was throwing firecrackers as it was just after Chinese New Year. So stupid me stood up and moved forward to help the women thinking some brat (there are many brats) was throwing firecrackers. My Khmer wife knew what it was and without me knowing had quickly whisked the children into the restaurant kitchen behind a brick wall and then come back for me. What had happened? Two robbers on motorbikes had tried to rob the young women's expensive motorbike and had followed her. A security guard (off duty police or soldier) had seen this and shot at the robbers. They returned the fire and in the end one robber was dead. No one else was hurt. BUT here we were with bullets flying past us no further than 4 meters away.

- **DO** also note that snatch and grab robbers on motorbikes are a growing problem. **DON'T** wear expensive obvious jewellery such as necklaces and handbags and mobile phones clipped onto your belt that can he grabbed. We have been robbed twice by such motorbike thieves. Again my wife saved me (she has saved my life at least 3 times and once negotiated with an armed robber who came into our house and demanded $1,000 or he would kill us). The story goes like this: I was driving our motorbike with my wife and child on the back (a favourite target for robbers) She heard a motor coming too close and changing down gears so she quickly changed the phone to another hand on the side away from the robbers and they grabbed a bag carrying a baby's nappy. My wife's reaction was surprising. She said we must get home as the robbers, finding only a nappy, will be angry and come back to beat us up for inconveniencing them. I felt like participating in some street justice myself! Some women have been pulled from the back of motorbikes when thieves on other bikes grabbed their bags or rucksack. If in a cyclo you are more at risk as they are so slow that robbers can easily grab your belongings even if you are wearing them.

- **DO** watch the moneyed toughs in expensive nightclubs. One of the annoying things on the dance floor of some of the more expensive Phnom Penh clubs are the brat sons of the rich and powerful. They are easily recognised by their arrogance, conspicuous shows of wealth, fashionable clothes and clumsy dancing that demands they are given all the dance floor. They will have bodyguards with guns who have been known to stick them in your face when you bump into their lads. Don't knock their hairstyle, right!!! If you cross them **DO** be wary if later, you meet them outside in the car park. Two Japanese tourists were badly stabbed with broken bottles when they refused to leave their seats at a food stall. Others have been shot when fights broke out. The Prime Minister is trying to control these rich thugs but they are still around. **DO** be careful and watch yourself if returning late at night especially in the back streets.

• **DON'T** take rides with drivers of new expensive bikes, especially if they speak good English. They are most certainly going to charge you more than the going rate and they are more likely to be robbers. It is safer to take a ride with an older non-English speaking man with an older bike.